NEWFOU
AND LAB
BOOK OF
Everything

Everything you wanted to know about
Newfoundland and Labrador and were
going to ask anyway

Martha Walls

MACINTYRE PURCELL PUBLISHING INC.

MacIntyre Purcell Publishing Inc.
232 Lincoln St., Suite D
PO Box 1142
Lunenburg, Nova Scotia
B0J 2C0
(902) 640-3350
www.bookofeverything.com
info@bookofeverything.com

Cover photo courtesy of 123RF.
Inside photo's provided by Istockphoto, 123RF, and Stock.xchng.
Joey Smallwood photo: National Archives of Canada PA-128080
Great Big Sea photo: courtesy Great Big Sea

Printed and bound in Canada by UGS.

Library and Archives Canada Cataloguing in Publication.
Newfoundland And Labrador Book Of Everything: Everything You Wanted To Know About Newfoundland And Labrador And Were Going To Ask Anyway / Martha Walls.
ISBN 978-0-9784784-4-5
1. Newfoundland and Labrador--Miscellanea. I. Title.
FC2161.W35 2006 971.8 C2006-903322-6

First published: 2006
Revised and Updated: 2008

Introduction

Of course no book can truly be about everything, but we hope the *Newfoundland and Labrador Book of Everything* captures something of the essence of this wonderful place. This is a book written by Newfoundlanders and Labradorians for the people who live here. Some of the information, we know, is stuff that will be familiar, but there will be lots you didn't know, and more still of what you didn't know you wanted to know.

We started this project with a single guiding principle — to write a book that was interesting, useful and, most importantly, entertaining. It should come as little surprise to anybody that we truly could have filled volumes. Unfortunately, some really interesting material was left on the cutting room floor. To this we say, "next time."

We think there is no book about Newfoundland and Labrador more comprehensive. There is no book more fun. Newfoundlander and Labradorians voted with their pocketbooks and turned the first edition released two years ago into a national bestseller. Well, we are back, and we think bigger and better than ever.

The compilation of this book was the product of much teamwork. Samantha Amara and Alisha Morrissey tackled a colossal amount of the research, writing and editing the first time around. Kelly Inglis managed and edited the revised addition, while Sandy Newton cheerfully tackled the new research, writing and editing as well.

Those who very generously took part in the Take Fives provided us with interesting, sometimes peculiar, and always entertaining insight into Newfoundland and Labrador. We had a lot of fun putting this book together. We hope you have as much fun reading it.

Martha Walls, May 2008

Table of Contents

Ode to Newfoundland

Sir Cavendish Boyle, Governor of Newfoundland from 1901 to 1904, penned the *Ode to Newfoundland*, as a testament to his love and affection for his adopted island home. It served as the national anthem from 1907 (the year Newfoundland became an independent Dominion) until Confederation in 1949. In 1980 the ode became the provincial anthem, making Newfoundland and Labrador the only province in the country to have one.

When sun rays crown thy pine clad hills,
And summer spreads her hand,
When silvern voices tune thy rills,
We love thee, smiling land.
We love thee, we love thee,
We love thee, smiling land.

When spreads thy cloak of shimmering white,
At winter's stern command,
Thro' shortened day, and starlit night,
We love thee, frozen land.
We love thee, we love thee
We love thee, frozen land.

As blinding storm gusts fret thy shore,
And wild waves lash thy strand,
Thro' spindrift swirl, and tempest roar,
We love thee windswept land.
We love thee, we love thee
We love thee windswept land.

As loved our fathers, so we love,
Where once they stood, we stand;
Their prayer we raise to Heaven above,
God guard thee, Newfoundland
God guard thee, God guard thee,
God guard thee, Newfoundland

Newfoundland and Labrador:

A Timeline

9000 Before Present: First people inhabit southern Labrador after glaciers retreat. Their descendants probably crossed to the Island of Newfoundland about 5000 BP.

1000 AD: Norse "Vikings" land near Black Duck Brook at L'Anse aux Meadows. Artifacts unearthed in the early 1960s support theories of brief settlement.

1497: Italian explorer John Cabot, sailing under the English flag, reaches the east coast of Newfoundland. Cabot claims the 'new founde land' for England.

1583: Sir Humphrey Gilbert arrives in Newfoundland with letters from Queen Elizabeth I authorizing him to stake the territory in her name and reiterating Cabot's previous claim.

1610: Looking to strengthen England's position in North America, the London and Bristol Company sends John Guy and 48 colonists to settle at Cupids.

1620: Sir George Calvert is granted land on the Avalon Peninsula. Three years later the royal Charter of Avalon secures these rights and titles to more land between Ferryland and Petty Harbour, over to Placentia Bay and up to Conception Bay. He calls his territory the Province of Avalon.

1662: Plaisance (now Placentia), a French capital, is founded with a governor and 80 settlers when King Louis XIV decides fortification and colonization are needed to protect French fishing grounds.

Skraelings Meet The Vikings

For centuries, Norse sagas offered clues that Vikings had visited North America long before Columbus "discovered" it in 1492. In the 1960s, Helge and Anne Stine Ingstad's archaeological findings at L'Anse aux Meadows on the northernmost tip of the Northern Peninsula showed that the Norse encountered the province's First People five centuries before European fishermen dropped anchor off the coast.

The archaeological findings offered evidence of an ancient Norse settlement dating to about 1000 AD, the year Leif Eriksson came ashore somewhere along North America's east coast. Debate surrounds the precise location of this landing, but the L'Anse aux Meadows discovery confirms Viking settlement; some believe that Newfoundland may have been the site of the Viking's "Vinland."

A second group of Viking settlers with as many as 135 men and 15 women spent several summers at L'Anse aux Meadows gathering wood and pelts that were in much demand in Greenland. On these visits the Vikings met, and for a time traded with, local people. Known to the Vikings as Skraelings, they were most likely Beothuk or Innu.

For unknown reasons, however, relations soured. Outnumbered by the unwelcoming Skraelings, the Vikings returned to Greenland, having spent fewer than five years in North America.

1696: After decades of shifting control between the French, British and Dutch, St. John's falls to French forces led by Pierre le Moyne, Sieur d'Iberville.

1699: King William's Act is the first British legislation applied to Newfoundland. It creates the fishing admiralty system of government.

1713: With the Treaty of Utrecht, France surrenders all of Newfoundland to England except for the French Shore on the north and west coasts.

1729: Naval Captain Henry Osborne is appointed the colony's first English governor.

1763: The Treaty of Paris ends the Seven Years' War and, with it, French claims to North America. France retains St. Pierre and Miquelon and the right to catch and dry fish along Newfoundland's French Shore, providing French fishermen leave the colony each season by September 10.

1791: The British Parliament passes legislation to create the first civil court in the colony. John Reeves is appointed Newfoundland's first judge and, in 1792, its first Chief Justice.

1816: The first of several major fires sweeps through St. John's, leaving more than a thousand people homeless.

1824: The British Parliament restricts the powers of Newfoundland's surrogate courts, repeals the authority of fishing admirals, and establishes a permanent Supreme Court with civil and criminal jurisdiction, on- and offshore.

1829: With the death of Shanawdithit, Newfoundland's aboriginal Beothuk peoples are recognized as being extinct.

1832: Newfoundland gets its first representative government; an elected House of Assembly and a Crown-appointed executive branch. The local legislature opens under Governor Sir Thomas John Cochrane.

1834: The new legislature creates the Savings Bank and allows the treasury to issue notes. The notes are recalled by 1857 but the bank prospers until it is sold to the Bank of Montreal in 1962.

1850: The Colonial Building, on Military Road in St. John's, is opened for the first time. It houses the provincial parliament until 1960.

1854: The Union Bank of Newfoundland is opened and incorporated. It is so successful that in 1857 it forces the closure of the Bank of British North America.

1855: Newfoundland gets full responsible government; Executive Council members are now appointed from the elected members of the House of Assembly.

1863: Legislation establishes the colony's money as dollars and cents, with the first one-, five-, ten-, twenty- and two-hundred-cent coins being issued in 1865.

1866: The 4,828 km-long Atlantic cable, laid from Ireland by the steamship *The Great Eastern*, is landed at Heart's Content — the first telegraph link between Europe and North America.

1869: Unsure of whether a union with other British colonies will raise or lower taxes, improve services, or debilitate the economy, Newfoundland votes "no" to joining the Canadian federation.

1881: The Newfoundland Railway Company begins construction of the first railway line, intended to link St. John's and Halls Bay (near present-day South Brook). Plans include a branch line to Harbour Grace.

1885: The St. John's Electric Light Company builds the colony's first generating station (the Flavin Lane Station) for the Terra Nova Bakery. In October, Newfoundlanders' eyes light up along with the display windows of 11 Water Street merchants.

1892: A carelessly dropped pipe, a stable full of hay, and a poorly timed closure of the city's water supply culminate in the Great Fire. The inferno rages through St. John's, destroying most of the city. More than 11,000 people are left homeless.

1895: Bell Island's iron ore mines open and remain in operation until 1966. During that period, over 80 million tonnes of ore are produced for a global market.

1895: Newfoundland, on the brink of bankruptcy, considers joining the Canadian federation, but a last-minute loan deftly negotiated by Sir Robert Bond saves the colony and Newfoundland again votes "no."

1898: The first mail and passenger train crosses Newfoundland from St. John's to Port-aux-Basques in June. The last passenger train will run the line in 1969; the last freight train in 1988.

1901: Guglielmo Marconi successfully receives the first transatlantic radio signal on Signal Hill in St. John's. It was sent from Ireland, 3,400 km away, and proved radio waves would follow the curvature of the Earth.

1904: The French give up all rights to the French Shore, retaining the islands of St. Pierre and Miquelon and rights to fish Newfoundland waters.

1908: The Fishermen's Protective Union (FPU) is established and spawns a political party. The FPU fares well in the 1913 election but the demands and political complications of Newfoundland's participation in the Great War destroys its momentum.

1915: A vote held on the total prohibition of the sale and consumption of alcohol receives about 5,000 votes more than needed to enact the ban. Prohibition becomes law in 1917.

1919: John Alcock and Arthur Whitten Brown leave St. John's and fly 3,041.7 km in just under 16 and a half hours to land in Clifden, Ireland, completing the first flight across the North Atlantic.

1923: The Salvation Army helps open the Grace Hospital, Newfoundland's first maternity facility.

1925: The Newfoundland Hotel, which costs an estimated $1 million, opens for business. Modern and impressive, the edifice reflects a new social and economic period in St. John's.

1927: The Judicial Committee of the English Privy Council settles the Labrador Boundary dispute between Quebec and Newfoundland, though Quebec still does not agree.

1933: Newfoundland is again on the brink of bankruptcy. Still unconvinced about joining Canada, Newfoundland asks Britain for help and trades its elected assembly for a Crown-appointed commission.

1948: Newfoundlanders must choose between a reformed Commission Government, the pre-1933 constitution, and joining the Canadian federation. After two referendums, a slim majority of Newfoundlanders favour confederation.

1949: On March 31, Newfoundland becomes Canada's tenth province.

1949: Joey (Joseph Roberts) Smallwood becomes leader of the provincial Liberal Party and Premier of the new province. His anti-confederate opponents become members of the Progressive Conservatives (PC).

1954: The government of Newfoundland and Labrador begins an outport resettlement program. By 1975, 40,000 people and 250 communities have been relocated.

1972: After 22 years and six election wins, Smallwood is relieved of his duties. Conservative (PC) Frank D. Moores becomes the second premier.

1974: After seven years and nearly a billion dollars, the electric power station at Churchill Falls in Labrador is complete.

1979: The Hibernia oilfield, the fifth largest discovered in Canada, is identified off the Grand Banks.

1979: Brian Peckford, PC, becomes the province's third premier.

1989: Thomas Rideout, another PC, becomes Newfoundland's fourth premier. His tenure is short — after one month he is defeated by Clyde Wells' Liberals in a general election.

1991: Joey Smallwood dies at home in St. John's.

1992: Ottawa places a moratorium on the cod fishery because of declining stocks. The move is intended as a short-term solution, but is extended indefinitely in 1993.

1993: Significant deposits of nickel, copper and cobalt are discovered at Voisey's Bay in Labrador. Inco, one of the world's largest nickel companies, acquires rights in 1996.

Outport Resettlement

Outports — small, isolated coastal fishing communities — were the first places Europeans settled here and are the oldest European communities in Canada. In the mid-20th century, however, steps were taken to dismantle these centuries-old villages.

In 1954, the provincial government began to relocate outport residents to "growth centres." In 1965, the federal government became a partner in the scheme, believing that relocated Newfoundlanders would earn better livelihoods and have easier access to social services. Cash payments in return for compliance proved a powerful incentive to cash-strapped fishers; by 1975, 250 outports had been abandoned. Almost 40,000 people, roughly 10 percent of the Newfoundland population, had been resettled.

By the late 1970s, critics were calling resettlement a failure. Unable to secure fishing licences in growth centres where fishing grounds had long been allocated, relocated families were caught in a web of unemployment. Homesick for the communities their ancestors had called home for generations, many former residents began to return to their coastal villages.

1996: Brian Tobin resigns as federal Minister of Fisheries to become leader of the province's Liberal party and premier.

1997: The oil platform at Hibernia, the largest in the world, begins producing. At 224 m tall, the platform is half as high as the Empire State Building, and more than 30 m taller than the Calgary Tower.

2000: Deputy premier Beaton Tulk becomes premier when Brian Tobin heads back to Ottawa and federal politics. He holds office for nearly four months until Roger Grimes is sworn in.

2001: An amendment to the Constitution of Canada officially changes the name of the province to "Newfoundland and Labrador."

2003: After twelve years of Liberal rule, PC Danny Williams is elected as the province's ninth premier.

2005: A comprehensive new deal is reached with Ottawa on sharing of offshore revenue. It is hailed as an economic turning point for the province.

2006: A small cod fishery is reopened for the first time since 1992, allowing a 2,500 tonne catch. The move is in response to fishers' anecdotal evidence of increased stocks. Scientists remain unconvinced of cod-stock recovery.

2006: In late June, citizens are appalled by Auditor General John Noseworthy's revelations about millions of dollars misused by elected representatives of all three parties over the previous decade.

BEST KEPT SECRETS OF LIVING WELL IN NL

"JAMB" is four Newfoundlanders who recognize a good thing when they see it. They are known individually (some far and wide) as John Baird, Andy Jones, Mary Lynn Bernard, and Brenda O'Brien. Says Mark Ferguson, curator of history at The Rooms Provincial Museum (a CFA — come-from-away — who married into the group and strong-armed it into revealing a few ways to feel great in a harsh place), "the answer appears to be make it simple, naturally."

1. **Enjoy a swim in the cold North Atlantic:** Yeah, but don't plunge in just anywhere: the secret is finding a sandy beach with a warm stream running into it. JAMB recommends Northern Bay Sands, Salmon Cove, Burgeo, or Windmill Bight.

2. **Take a trip to a resettled community:** There are boat tours to islands in Placentia or Trinity Bays, and in some places (such as British Harbour, TB) you can hike in. Sit, be quiet, reflect, have a boil-up — but leave the place as you found it: quiet, but speaking volumes.

3. **Eat fresh:** Forget what you learned about fish from growing up on the mainland — if you can get ultra-fresh cod, pan-fried and golden, your taste buds have a ticket to heaven. Keep your eye out for a place that adds fresh chanterelles to the meal, and you're over the moon. If you can't find a spot that takes this approach, at least ask a local for the best place to get fish and chips. You must not visit the province without having a good fish experience.

4. **Head immediately for the coast when someone says the capelin are rolling:** It's the thing to do and everyone knows it. Some take their buckets to get a feed, others go to watch the humpbacks chase the capelin almost onto the strand — and the rest are there just because it's where the action is, only once a year. Capelin roll all around the coast when the season (and the beach) is right. In season (June or July), one of the best spots on the Avalon to watch humpbacks from shore is the long gravel stretch by St. Vincent's, where they lunge after capelin only a few metres from shore.

5. **Pat a Newfoundland pony:** They're tiny, they're sweet, and there aren't very many of them. Say hello, when you get a chance.

2006: Skip Brad Gushue, a 25-year-old Newfoundlander, leads the Canadian men's curling team (with second Russ Howard, third Mark Nichols, and lead Jamie Korab) to its first-ever Olympic curling gold — the first Newfoundland and Labrador-based athletes ever to win the top Olympic medal.

2007: Premier Danny Williams's Conservative government is re-elected by a landslide, winning 43 of 47 seats in the House of Assembly. They receive the highest vote share — 69.5 percent — since Joey Smallwood's 70 percent in 1949.

2007: The saga of Fishery Products International, the mega-company created in 1983 and supported by the provincial and federal governments to strengthen the fishing industry, nears a close with the announcement that the government has authorized the sale of FPI assets to Ocean Choice International and High Liner Foods.

Newfoundland and Labrador Essentials

Origin of Name: Drawing on the Italian term *terra nova*, or 'New Land,' John Cabot named Newfoundland in 1497. The origin of the name Labrador is more of a mystery. Most concur that the name originated with 16th century Portuguese explorer João Fernades, who was a wealthy landowner, which in Portuguese is a *lavrador*. At Confederation in 1949, the newly minted, two-part province was known simply as Newfoundland, but an amendment to the Canadian Constitution in 2001 officially changed the name to Newfoundland and Labrador.

Capital City: St. John's

Licence Plate: "A World of Difference" first appeared on the Newfoundland and Labrador license plate in 1993. In 1996, commemoration plates were issued to mark the 500th anniversary of Cabot's landing that was celebrated in 1997.

Nickname: "The Rock" — so named for the province's rocky glacial landscapes and craggy coast.

Motto: *Quaerite prime regnum Dei*, which means "Seek ye first the Kingdom of God."

Provincial Flag: Officially adopted in 1980 — more than three decades after the province joined confederation — the flag's four blue Union Jack-like triangles reflect its Commonwealth heritage. Two larger triangles are outlined in red representing the island and the mainland portions of the province. The golden arrow points toward a bright future. A white background symbolizes ice and snow; blue the sea, and red, human efforts. It was designed by artist Christopher Pratt.

Provincial Flower: The Pitcher Plant, first chosen by Queen Victoria to grace the Newfoundland penny, was named official flower in 1954. Found in bogs and marshes, the plant's leaves trap insects, turning them into much needed sustenance in these nutrient-deficient habitats.

Tartan: Registered in 1973, the tartan features gold, white, brown and red on a green background. The colours represent the sun's rays, the cloak of snow, the iron historically mined on Bell Island, the Royal Standard and the pine hills.

Take 5 TOP FIVE LANGUAGES

THAT NEWFOUNDLANDERS AND LABRADORIANS CLAIM AS A MOTHER TONGUE, OTHER THAN ENGLISH:

1. **French** (0.42%)
3. **Chinese** (0.15%)
4. **German** (0.14%)
4. **Inuktituk** (0.13%)
5. **Arabic** (0.12%)

Source: Statistics Canada.

Coat of Arms: King Charles I granted Newfoundland its coat of arms in 1637. The cross on the crest is based on the red cross of St. George (as featured on the flag of England), though the cross here is white. In the opposing quadrants sit two yellow lions and two white unicorns (both of them in England's coat of arms). Flanking each side of, and supporting the crest, are Beothuk warriors. The symbol boasts an elk above the crest. Below it, in Latin, is the provincial motto which comes from Matthew 7:23 of the New Testament. Forgotten over time, the coat of arms was unused for more than 250 years before being 'rediscovered' and adopted as the insignia of the Dominion of Newfoundland in 1928. The coat of arms remained after the province entered Confederation.

Provincial Bird: The Atlantic Puffin is the provincial bird. Approximately 95 percent of North America's estimated 350,000 pairs breed in colonies on the coasts of Newfoundland and Labrador.

Provincial Dog: An adept swimmer with strength and intelligence enough to pull drowning victims to safety, the Newfoundland Dog is a famed symbol of loyalty and devotion. It's believed the dog was first identified in Sir Thomas Bewick's 1790 nature tome *British Quadrupeds*, in which it was identified as a Newfoundland Dog in honour of its origin.

They Said It

"One of the Shawnees, a respectable looking Indian, offered me three beaver skins for my dog, with which he appeared much pleased; I prised much for his docility and qualifications generally for my journey and of course there was no bargain."
— Captain Meriwether Lewis, of his Newfoundland Dog that accompanied him and William Clark on their famed North American expedition of 1804-1806.

Provincial Tree: Common in the province, the black spruce has supported the province's pulp and paper industry. It was named the provincial tree in 1991.

Time Zone: Unique in North America, the time zone of the island of Newfoundland is a half hour ahead of the Atlantic time zone, on which most of Labrador operates.

System of Measurement: Metric

Voting Age: 18

Statutory Holidays: New Year's Day, Good Friday, Memorial Day (July 1), Labour Day and Christmas Day are the province's five official statutory holidays. Stores and offices are not required to close on St. Patrick's Day, St. George's Day, Victoria Day, Orangeman's Day or Thanksgiving Day, though many do on the nearest Monday.

POPULATION BREAKDOWN
- Total population of Newfoundland and Labrador: 505,469
- Population of Newfoundland: 479,105
- Population of Labrador: 26,364
- Capital City: St. John's, population 181,110
- Percentage of total population living in urban areas: 58
- Percentage of population living in rural areas: 42

Source: Statistics Canada.

POPULATION IN PERSPECTIVE
Geographically, Newfoundland and Labrador is nearly double the size of Great Britain, though the latter boasts over 112 times its population. While Japan is only slightly smaller, it has more than 127 million people. Echoing a trend common in the Atlantic region, the province's population is decreasing. A lack of immigration, the consistent out-

migration of Newfoundlanders looking for better opportunities else-where, and the lowest fertility rate in Canada, have conspired to cre-ate this downward trend.

Sources: Newfoundland and Labrador Tourism; Statistics Canada.

Take 5 IRIS BRETT'S TOP FIVE
FAVOURITE THINGS ABOUT OUTPORT LIFE

"I think my friends see me as reclusive, eccentric and stodgy. I think I am bright, witty and charming. I punched my time in the workforce as a dietician, school teacher, bank clerk, florist and editor and general dogsbody of our family-owned weekly newspaper, The Northern Reporter. Not all at the same time, but in that order. I retired in 1990 to plant potatoes and pick berries."

1. **The tallest building is two stories**. This leaves more room for the sky.

2. **My outport hugs the ocean**. The ocean provides no accommodation for mosquitoes, black flies or other flying blood-suckers.

3. **There are no "strangers."** An unfamiliar face must answer a standard string of questions designed to expose their pedigree within five minutes. The grapevine spreads the word before sundown.

4. **Any attempt at forming a social stratum is doomed to failure**. Even the clergyperson is expected to help paint the church.

5. **Everyone is a meteorologist accurately forecasting upcoming weather systems by observing the actions of birds and animals and other critters.** Did you know that when earthworms crawl on top of the ground, rain is not far away?

You Know You're From Newfoundland

- You don't think twice about stopping your pickup on the highway to talk out your window to a friend in his vehicle, who's heading the other way.
- You have a satellite dish with 500 channels and you still watch the NTV evening news.
- You know the shed and the barn are great places for people to drink and socialize.
- You love it when the service station gives you ten pounds of potatoes instead of a car wash when you fill your tank.
- You look for touton dough in the grocery store freezer when you want to make a pizza.
- You go out in shorts and t-shirts in March if the temperature's above 5°C.
- All traffic stops when you just look as if you want to cross the street.
- You're likely to think that cool, foggy weather is "some sultry, b'y."
- You don't go "fishing" for trout, you go trouting, of course.
- You catch your trout in a gully, which a mainlander might call a river.
- Your favourite restaurant has staff that treat you like family, endearments ("me duckie") and all.
- "Bike" means an all-terrain vehicle, and most people you know own at least one.
- You know where the best free places to sleep on the Gulf ferries are, and you try to nab them as soon as you get on board.
- You know what a beef bucket is, and you've had more jiggs dinners than you can count.
- You consider flipper pie a seasonal treat.
- You've experienced every known weather phenomenon in a single day.
- At least one of your relatives works at Hibernia or in Alberta.
- You voted for the less-talented person on Canadian Idol, just because they were from Newfoundland.

and Labrador When . . .

- You know that "me son" is not a term of parenthood, but "me mudder" is.
- You understand what the "Mount Pearl Curl" is and you've either had one or seen one.
- You plan your driving around the times when moose are most likely to be on the road.
- You switch from "heat" to "A/C" and back again in the same day.
- You know driving is better in the winter because all the pot-holes are filled with snow.
- You think everyone from the rest of Canada has an accent.
- Orangeman's Day and Bonfire Night are important party nights on your yearly calendar.
- You know the difference between "baymen" and "townies."
- You know the words to at least one song by "Buddy Wasisname and the Other Fellers."
- Your idea of a traffic jam is ten cars waiting to pass a back-hoe on the highway.
- It takes 3 hours to go downtown for one item because you meet half the people you know and you have to stop and talk.
- You only use two spices—salt and ketchup.
- You owe more money on your snowblower than your car.
- You have several favourite recipes for bottled moose.
- You've taken your kids trick-or-treating in a blizzard before.
- You know who Snook is, and you know someone just like him.
- Most parties you go to are either held in the kitchen or eventually end up there.
- You know what a Mickey and 2-4 are, and have often brought them to parties.
- You talk about the weather with strangers and friends alike.
- Community names like "Cranky Point," "Joe Batt's Arm" or "Dildo" don't strike you as all that funny.

They Said It

NOT IN THE MILLION CLUB

The population of Newfoundland and Labrador is not likely to break the million mark, according to current projections. Between 1979 and 2003, 50,000 people, a full nine percent of the province's population, pulled up stakes and headed west. In only four of the last 45 years have newcomers outnumbered those who chose to leave the province. The biggest exodus occurred between 1994 and 1999, thanks to the collapse of the cod fishery; in 1998 alone, 12,000 Newfoundlanders and Labradorians left. In 2007, the population of the province was still declining (due in part to a higher death rate than birth rate), but it received a boost late in the year; from July to October 3,078 people left the province, but 4,162 moved to it.

Sources: Newfoundland and Labrador Statistics Agency; Newfoundland and Labrador Department of Finance.

POPULATION DENSITY (KM²)

- Canada: 3.5
- Newfoundland and Labrador: 1.4
- St. John's: 225.1
- Toronto: 3,972
- Vancouver: 5,039
- New York City: 10,194
- Tokyo: 5,751

Sources: Statistics Canada 2006 Census; US Census 2000, Statistics Handbook of Japan 2007.

Take 5 TOP FIVE LARGEST CITIES AND TOWNS

1. **St. John's:** 181,110
2. **Corner Brook:** 26,628
3. **Mount Pearl:** 24,671
4. **Conception Bay South:** 21,966
5. **Grand Falls-Windsor:** 13,558

Source: Statistics Canada.

IN WITH THE TIDE

Like the other Atlantic provinces, Newfoundland and Labrador attracts relatively few immigrants. Of the 8,380 immigrants living in the province, nearly half are from Europe, 23 percent are from the Americas, and 21 percent come from Asia. Just under 7.5 percent hail from other regions, including Africa and Oceania.

Source: Statistics Canada.

Did you know...

that until the late 20th century, St. John's was the only officially designated city in Newfoundland and Labrador?

Did you know...

that St. John's is the only city in the country with radio stations whose call letters do not begin with the letter "C", the International Telecommunication Union (ITU) prefix for Canada? ITU prefixes for the Dominion of Newfoundland were "VO" and three AM stations in the province kept their existing call letters after 1949.

BOYS AND GIRLS
Population by Age and Sex

Age	Males	Females	Total
0-14	39,436	37,161	76,597
15-24	32,479	32,032	64,511
25-44	66,784	70,999	137,783
45-64	77,409	79,406	156,815
65+	31,692	38,877	70,569

Median Age

Men: 39.7   Women: 41.3   Both: 40.5

- By 2018, the median age is expected to increase to 49.2.

Life Expectancy

Newfoundland and Labrador males: 75.4
Newfoundland and Labrador females: 80.9
Canadian males: 77.8
Canadian females: 82.6

Did you know...

that Newfoundland and Labrador has the least farmland of any province?

CRADLE TO GRAVE

- Births (yearly): 4,326
- Deaths (yearly): 4,549
- Fertility Rate (number of children a woman will have during her lifetime): The country's lowest at 1.3

Take 5 JOAN RITCEY'S TOP FIVE
ESSENTIAL READS

Joan Ritcey is a librarian with Memorial University Libraries and the head of its Centre for Newfoundland Studies. She is editor of the *Newfoundland Periodical Article Bibliography*, an index to 80,000 NL periodical articles on Newfoundland and Labrador.

1. **Peter E. Pope's** *Fish into Wine: The Newfoundland plantation in the seventeenth century.* Chapel Hill: University of North Carolina Press, 2004. 463 pages.

2. **Ingeborg Marshall's** *The History and Ethnography of the Beothuk*. McGill-Queen's, 1996. 640 pages.

3. **Patrick O'Flaherty's** *Old Newfoundland: A history to 1843* and *Lost Country: The rise and fall of Newfoundland 1843-1933.* St. John's: Long Beach Press, 2005. 2 volumes.

4. *The Dictionary of Newfoundland English*, **edited by G.M. Story, W.J. Kirwin and J.D.A. Widdowson.** Toronto: University of Toronto Press, 1998.

5. **David Macfarlane's** *The Danger Tree: Memory, war and the search for a family's past*. Toronto: Vintage Canada, 2000. 307 pages.

Take 5 **TOP FIVE RELIGIONS**

THAT NEWFOUNDLANDERS AND LABRADORIANS ADHERE TO AFTER ROMAN CATHOLICISM AND PROTESTANT FAITHS

1. **Christian Orthodox and other Christians**
2. **Muslim**
3. **Hindu**
4. **Buddhist**
5. **Jewish**

Source: Statistics Canada.

MARRIAGE

- Rate of marriage in Newfoundland and Labrador (per 1,000 population): 5.5
- Marriage rate in Nunavut, Canada's lowest: 2.3
- Marriage rate in Quebec, next lowest: 2.8
- Marriage rate in Prince Edward Island, Canada's highest: 6.0
- National marriage rate: 4.7
- Age of groom at first marriage in Newfoundland and Labrador: 29.9
- Age of bride at first marriage: 28.0

Source: Statistics Canada.

Did you know...

that married couples formed 73.6 percent of the census families in 2006 — the second highest rate behind Ontario (73.9 percent)?

Higher Education

Memorial University of Newfoundland and Labrador (MUN):
Founded in 1925 as Memorial University College, MUN was granted university status in 1949. It is the largest university in Atlantic Canada, with 17,500 undergraduate and graduate students engaged in full- and part-time studies at campuses in St. John's (main campus and Marine Institute), in Corner Brook (Sir Wilfred Grenfell College), and in Harlow, England. The university employs 950 full-time faculty (and 850 sessional instructors) and 2,300 administrative and support staff.

The College of the North Atlantic: Newfoundland and Labrador's public college can trace its beginnings to 1963 and the decade after, during which 17 District Vocational Schools opened around the province. These institutions underwent various changes in character and name, and several amalgamations, over the next 25 years. In 1997 CNA was formed from the five community colleges then in existence. The College of the North Atlantic now has 17 campuses in the province and one in Doha, Qatar, in the Middle East. It offers nearly 100 full-time programs and more than 300 part-time courses to some 20,000 students each year.

Academy Canada: Founded in 1985, Academy Canada is eastern Canada's largest independent college, with three campuses (the original one in Corner Brook and two in St. John's) and a student population of more than 1,100. It offers career-based training, both academic and practical, in some 40 programs ranging from American Sign Language/Deaf Studies and Animal Grooming to Travel/Tourism/Hospitality and Welding.

Keyin College: Founded in 1980, Keyin College now has nine campuses on the Island and more than 25,000 graduates. Its industry-driven curriculum offers 32 programs of study: these include Aquaculture, Early Childhood Education, and Human Resources Management, as well as training for such jobs as Medical Transcriptionist, Funeral Director/Embalmer, and Pharmacy Technician.

CompuCollege: The St. John's campus of CompuCollege opened in 1985, and since then has graduated more than 5,000 students. It currently offers a dozen programs of study, with a focus on training for careers in information technology and business. The average annual enrolment of the college is approximately 250.

Did you know...

that the fishing village of Renews on the Avalon Peninsula once served as a pit stop for the Pilgrims' *Mayflower*? During the ship's 66-day voyage to Plymouth Rock in 1620, it docked at Renews to pick up water and supplies to complete its journey.

D-I-V-O-R-C-E

- Divorce rate in Newfoundland and Labrador (per 100,000): 146
- Divorce rate in North West Territories, the lowest: 117
- Divorce rate in Yukon, the highest: 319
- Divorce rate in Canada: 223

Source: Department of Justice Canada.

AGE STRUCTURE

- Percentage of population that is under 25: 27.9
- Age 25 to 44: 27.2
- Age 45 to 64: 31
- Age 65 and over: 13.9

Source: Statistics Canada.

FAMILY STRUCTURE

- Percentage of children living in married two-parent households: 65.5
- Percentage of children living in common law, two-parent families: 8.7
- Percentage of children living in female lone-parent families: 21.1
- Percentage of children living in male lone-parent families: 4.7

Source: Statistics Canada.

Did you know...

that Water Street in St. John's, first used in the early 1500s, is the oldest commercial street in North America?

RELIGIOUS AFFILIATION

Religiously, Newfoundland and Labrador is divided along Catholic and Protestant lines. While about half of St. John's belong to the Roman Catholic Church, nearly 60 percent of the province's population is Protestant. Together, Catholics and Protestants account for over 96 percent of the faithful.

HEALTH CARE PROFESSIONALS

- Physicians (General Practice): 519
- Physicians (Specialists): 526
- Registered Nurses: 6,349
- Licensed Practical Nurses: 2,686
- Dentists: 166
- Pharmacists: 591

Sources: Newfoundland and Labrador Department of Health and Community Services; Canadian Institute for Health Information; NL Pharmacy Board; Provincial Dentist Registry Authority.

EDUCATION

In 2006/7, the province had:

- 5 school boards
- 285 public schools
- 74,304 students
- 5,444.5 teachers

Source: NL Department of Education Statistics.

Did you know...

that Newfoundland and Labrador has the highest proportion — more than 50 percent — of young adults (20 to 29) living in the parental home? The national average is 43.5 percent.

FULL-TIME STUDENTS ENROLLED

Universities: 12,809 (MUN, both campuses)
Graduate programs and medicine: 1,834
Colleges (Provincial): 6,697 (17 campuses)
Other (private) colleges: 2,892
Public schools: 74,304
Private or independent schools: 131

Sources: MUN Fact Book 2006, NL Dept. of Education, NL Statistics, Independent Schools Directory.

COMMUNICATIONS

Daily/weekly newspapers: 20
TV/cable broadcasting source stations: 4
AM / FM radio stations: 35

Sources: MUN Library, Atlantic Canada Newspapers, CRTC.

Weblinks

Centre for Newfoundland Studies

www.library.mun.ca/qeii/cns/cns_main.php

Maintained by the Centre for Newfoundland Studies, this website tells you how to access information housed at the centre and also provides an exhaustive list of links to websites concerning Newfoundland. Have a burning question about Newfoundland? Pose it here using the "Ask a Newfoundland Question" feature.

Newfoundland and Labrador Heritage

www.heritage.nf.ca

This website, maintained by various partners, provides vast amounts of information about the province's economic, political, cultural and natural history before and after the coming of Europeans.

Newfoundland and Labrador Tourism

www.newfoundlandandlabradortourism.com

For many more quick facts about the province, as well as a heads up as to things you must see when you visit, check out this website presented by the provincial government.

Place names

Place names provide us with clues about a region's history. They can reveal secrets about a place from days gone by, denote an important geographical feature (sometimes one lost to development), or tell us about the life and culture of the people who coined the name. Newfoundland and Labrador is peppered with place names that provide a rich treasure of historical markers.

Argentia: The former site of an American naval base, it's located in Placentia Bay and is a seasonal terminus for the Marine Atlantic ferry to North Sydney. It was originally known as Little Placentia — because it's next door to Placentia (originally Plaisance), the former French capital of Newfoundland, whose name means "pleasant." It was renamed Argentia after a silver deposit was found there in 1904.

Bakeapple Bay: This Labrador town's namesake is the locally abundant marsh plant, which has been used to treat scurvy as well as to make tasty preserves.

Bareneed: First called either Barren Head, after the shore's desolate hilltops, or Bearing Head, as a marker for those travelling on the sea, the dialect of this Avalon town's early settlers is blamed for the linguistic corruption.

Barking Kettle Pond: This common name for a small pond or other location near a community comes from the traditional practice of treating sails and nets in a concoction of conifer bark and buds boiled in a huge kettle. "Barking" was known as a "great preservative" as early as 1795.

Black Joke Cove: Legends say this cove provided perfect cover for the notorious pirate ship *Black Joke* to lay in wait to raid passing merchant ships.

Bonavista: This is where John Cabot first laid eyes on Newfoundland and reportedly exclaimed, "Oh, Happy Sight!" or in his native Italian, *"O Buono Vista!"* A windy and barren locale, Bonavista is nevertheless quite close to important fishing and sealing grounds, and so became the place to fish for the Spanish, Portuguese, French and English during the 1500s.

Blow Me Down: Blow-me-downs are steep hills or bluffs rising sharply out of the water. They can produce sudden downdrafts that may blow down vessels that approach too close. Many places in the province bear the name.

Butter Pot Hill: Found throughout the province, "butter pots" are rounded rocky hills that resemble old-fashioned butter pots. The province's highest rises 303 m above sea level in Butter Pot Provincial Park near St. John's.

Cape Onion: At the tip of the Island's Northern Peninsula, this cape is named not for the way it smells, but for its shape. Early maps show the name as Cape Dognon, a perversion of the French word for the pungent vegetable.

Cape White Handkerchief: Not the site of a massive surrender, this cape at the entrance to Nachvak Fiord in Labrador welcomes those who approach by the sea with a large face of light-coloured rock.

Castors River: The name of this western locale comes from *castor*, French for beaver.

Cavendish: Originally called Shoal Bay, the name was changed in 1905 to memorialize and celebrate Sir Cavendish Boyle, Newfoundland governor from 1901 to 1904 and author of the provincial anthem "Ode to Newfoundland."

Clarenville: It's thought that the town was named after the eldest son of the Prince of Wales — the Duke of Clarence — and was originally called Clarenceville. Since there is no proof of when settlers first landed in Clarenville, there is no proof that's where the name came from.

Come By Chance: As early as 1714, this town was referred to as Comby Chance, and as Come-By-Chance by the mid 1830s. The French used the port as a staging area to plunder English settlements in Trinity Bay; historians feel the element of surprise in the raids inspired the name.

Conche: Although locals claim the town is named for the Caribbean conch shell, it is more likely named for the Abbey of Conches, founded by Roger de Toeni I (990-1039) in Normandy.

Corner Brook: The province's second largest community was named by Captain James Cook in 1767. A small community until the last century, Corner Brook grew exponentially in the 1920s thanks to the pulp and paper industry that remains its economic heart. Corner Brook received city status in 1981.

Cow Head: This peninsula on the west coast of the island was named for a prominent boulder (now gone) that resembled a cow's head. In 1534, Jacques Cartier named the same headland Cap Pointe.

St. John's: City of Legends

St. John's, the capital of Newfoundland and Labrador, is the province's most populous city. St. John's proper is home to just over 100,000 while the greater metro area boasts more than 180,000 residents.

Founded 500 years ago, the city is the oldest in North America. Italian Giovanni Caboto, a.k.a. John Cabot, is often cited as the first European to drop anchor in St. John's Harbour. Sponsored by English King Henry VII, Cabot arrived at St. John's on June 24, 1497, the feast day of Saint John the Baptist. By 1540, French, Basque and Portuguese ships were travelling to San Jehan each spring to exploit the teeming cod stocks off the Avalon Peninsula, though there are records that suggest they had a presence here even before Cabot.

In 1583, Sir Humphrey Gilbert stopped by and officially claimed Newfoundland for England, and by 1675 St. John's was the largest settlement in the colony, large enough to warrant a census. As the English, Dutch and French grappled for supremacy in the international fishery in the last half of the 17th century, control over St. John's shifted — sometimes violently — between these super-powers.

The British finally won the day, and after 1762 the heavily fortified city remained in British hands. Today, most natives claim either Irish and English heritage — or both. The earliest Europeans to settle the city came from southeastern Ireland, accounting for similarities in accents and dialects between the two regions. Today St. John's is a bustling metropolis. It is the second largest city in Atlantic Canada and serves as the business, education and government centre of Newfoundland and Labrador.

Cranky Point: Not a reference to the locals' demeanour, this place gets its name from the dangers of the sea that surround it. "Cranky" possibly stems from the English "crank" and/or the Dutch "krengd," both of which describe a boat that is easily heeled to a sharp angle by the wind. Many vessels experienced this when trying to navigate the waters around this windy point.

Cupids: Appointed in 1610 to settle a colony and secure the fishing trade, John Guy and 39 colonists made their way to this Trinity Bay site. Originally known as Cupers's Cove and corrupted over time to Cupitts, Coppers and Cubbits Cove, the colony was home to the first British child born in the province (in 1613, a boy). Ultimately, Guy's colony failed.

Cut Throat Island: The name of this Labrador site is not a link to pirates past, but to the province's fishing heritage. It comes from the term "cut-throater," the person in the process of preparing cod for salting who performed this task.

Dildo: Several theories explain the origin of this unusual name, from the harmless to the suggestive. By far the most interesting concerns the reputed sense of humour of Captain James Cook and his right hand man, Michael Lane. Both enjoyed "shock value," and since the word "dildo" had pretty much the same meaning back then as it does today, the duo could have applied the name to make the more sensitive blush.

Fleur de Lys: The most northerly village on the Baie Verte Peninsula lies beneath a large hill with three bumpy knolls that looks like a fleur-de-lis. In early days it was also called Flower de Luce.

Funk Island: Sometimes life just stinks, as it most always does here, where unimaginable numbers of seabirds congregate. The island first earned the name when it was a great auk breeding colony. The flightless birds and their eggs were harvested in huge numbers by European visitors and settlers, and are now extinct. The name could also derive from the Norse or Icelandic term for the big pile of hay it resembles.

Grand Falls-Windsor: This central town is actually two that amalgamated in 1991. Grand Falls, established as a lumber company town in 1905, was named after falls on the Exploits River. Windsor, its neighbour, was established around the railroad station and grew to accommodate those who did not work for the Anglo-Newfoundland Development Company.

Ha Ha Bay: Used five times in the province, the name probably stems from an Old French expression used to describe an unexpected obstruction or a dead end. In this Northern Peninsula locale, a sand bar prevents direct passage to Pistolet Bay.

Happy Adventure: A very relieved Captain George Holbrooke christened the cove after finding shelter there during a storm, or so the story goes.

Happy Valley-Goose Bay: Goose Bay was originally established as the site of Labrador's American military base (Goose Air Base) during World War II. A site about eight miles away called Refugee Cove, the site for non-military workers' housing, was renamed Happy Valley. The two towns amalgamated in 1975.

Heart's Content: Called "Hartes Content" as early as 1612, this community, as well as Heart's Delight, Heart's Desire, and possibly Little Heart's Ease, were likely named after ships.

Horse Islands: Oddly, no horses ever lived here. Folklorist P.K. Devine hints that the name derives from the white rolling waves that strike the land during a storm — such waves were called "white horses" by seamen.

Indian Tickle: A tickle is a narrow saltwater strait that is difficult to navigate, so the name peppers maps and charts of the province. In Labrador, Indian Tickle is a mainland community while across the tickle lies Indian Island, a summer fishing station.

Take 5 FIVE FREE THINGS TO DO
IN NEWFOUNDLAND AND LABRADOR

1. **Birdwatch:** Anywhere along the coast should give you a chance to spot sea- and shorebirds, not to mention icebergs. Headlands and tidal flats are particularly good birding locations.

2. **Watch whales:** From any headland on a clear day; on the Avalon, the long cobblestone beach near St. Vincent's (route #90, a.k.a. the Irish Loop) can, when the capelin are in, give you an exhilarating look at humpbacks up close.

3. **Walk or hike:** Almost every town or community has a walking path—consult the tourism guide or ask a local. In the capital city, the Grand Concourse network of trails threads throughout the city, and you can finish (or start) your perambulations with the spectacular view from the top of Signal Hill. The Avalon Peninsula's East Coast Trail covers 540 km of coastline.

4. **Pick berries in season:** Bakeapples, wild strawberries, blueberries, partridgeberries—anywhere that looks good or local knowledge suggests. Learn more about berries at Newfoundland and Labrador's first economuseum—Wild Berry Economusée run by the Dark Tickle jam makers—in Griquet, on the Great Northern Peninsula (admission is free).

5. **Visit The Rooms:** Located in St. John's, home of the Provincial Museum, Art Gallery, and Archives. Admission is free every Wednesday evening from 6:00 to 9:00, and the first Saturday of every month.

Ireland's Eye: This resettled community on an island of the same name in Trinity Bay could have been named by homesick settlers who believed they could see Ireland on a clear day. It may also memorialize an island of the same name in the Irish Sea.

Jerry's Nose: A sandy beach and a cliff flank this community that boasts a narrow projection that resembles a nose. Jerry could have been an early resident.

Joe Batts Arm: There are at least two theories about where this name came from. The community itself favours the story that in the early 1750s, when Captain James Cook was charting the waters around Newfoundland, a sailor named Joe Batt jumped ship and settled in the "arm" — another word for an inlet. It must have been a successful move, as the locale became known as "Joe Batt's Arm."

Kaumajet Mountains: The name of this Labrador mountain chain comes from the Inuit meaning "shining top" or "shining mountains," terms even more appropriate when the peaks are covered in snow.

Naked Man Hill: Named after a pile of stones erected by Captain Cook while surveying the coast, a practice used by many surveyors. From a distance, the structure appears human-shaped.

Oil Jacket Cove: This cove in French Bay was named for the waterproof jackets worn in the fishery, which were made by soaking garments, raw flour sacks, or canvas in raw linseed oil.

Pinchgut Point: This name on the shores of Placentia Bay is reminiscent of lean times on the sea and a scarcity of food. Similar names, such as Famish Gut, did not make the cut during the provincial government's place-name reform in the 1960s.

Quidi Vidi: No one really knows the root of this unique name. It's been through 25 different spellings and almost as many pronunciations but the accepted one is "kiddy viddy" or "quida vida."

St. Anthony: Located on the northernmost tip of the island of Newfoundland, St. Anthony was named in 1534 by Jacques Cartier. In early years it was also known as St. Anthony Haven, as it was a safe harbour near productive fishing grounds.

Newfoundland and Labrador Slang:

A Dictionary of Newfoundland English

Visitors find it peculiar, intoxicating and, at times, downright incomprehensible. But to Newfoundlanders and Labradorians, their language is much more. 'Newfoundland English' carries the thick remnants of Irish and English accents and expressions, binding the people of the province together with a sense of place and community that reaches centuries into the past.

'Angishore/hangashore: A man too lazy to fish; one who happily has no ambition or someone who is weak and sickly and deserves pity.

Beater: A harp seal that has just lost its white 'pup' coat and is on its way north from its birthplace on the ice floes off the coast.

In the Dawnies: Dawnies used to be used to mean 'nightmares' but today, 'being in the dawnies' means to be tuckered out or nursing oneself back to health the morning after the night before.

Berth: A coveted reserved bunk on a springtime sealing vessel. Having a berth was accompanied by a promise in a share of the hunt's profits.

Bivver: A shiver, shake or tremor, especially of the lips. The word also describes a buoy or some other floating object that barely breaks the water's surface.

Blow the Christmas Pudding: A term describing the boisterous and excited celebration of taking the Christmas pudding out of the pot to the accompaniment of gunfire.

Boil-up: A cup-a-tea and a snack enjoyed during a quick break from hard work on land or at sea.

Buddy: Colloquial nickname for any man whose name is unknown or forgotten, used especially when relating a tale about him.

Take 5 — DR. SANDRA CLARK'S FAVOURITE NEWFOUNDLAND EXPRESSIONS

Dr. Sandra Clarke, a native Newfoundlander, is a University Research Professor in the Department of Linguistics at Memorial University. One of her primary research interests is Newfoundland English.

In light of the many colourful expressions found in Newfoundland and Labrador English (some of which appear unique to our language variety, others of which also occur in a number of other places in the English-speaking world), it is difficult to pick a top five. The following are her personal choices, with input from a number of other people; an online search will show that most are identified as common Newfoundland and Labrador expressions by many current and former residents of the province.

1. **Stay where you're to and I'll come where you're at**. (Also appears as: Stay where you're at and I'll come where you're to.)
2. **Oh, me nerves!**
3. **Up she comes.**
4. **I dies at you.** (From "I dies laughing at you")
5. **Whaddya at?** (From "What are you doing"?)

Clumper: A small iceberg, especially one that has washed ashore.

Dory: A small boat with a flat bottom and high sides, sharp on both ends. This boat was designed for stability.

Duckish: A word to describe dark and gloomy light, such as at dusk.

Duff: A hearty pudding made of flour, water, suet and raisins. Boiled in a bag with an occasional drop of molasses, it was a perfect snack for hard-working sealers on a Sunday day of rest.

Figgy duff, bun, cake, etc.: Any of these items prepared with raisins. Figgy pudding is a favorite on Christmas Day, though preparation of it begins the day before.

Flipper dinner: The front flipper of a seal used by sealers to hoist the animal up onto the ice is used in a meal by those who consume the mammal (also known as flipper pie.)

Gaff: A type of boathook used for various fishing tasks and/or a hook on a longer pole used by sealers in the hunt.

Gaffer: A young, ambitious lad who is willing and able to help out in laborious tasks such as fishing or cutting wood.

Gommel: A simple-minded or stupid looking man.

Hag or old hag: A nightmare in which an old woman is seen pressing on the chest of the victim who cannot move under her imaginary weight. Also used for the uneaten inner organs of a lobster that are thrown away.

Heave out: A term used to describe the capsizing or rolling over of a ship.

Irish toothache: Nickname for a pregnancy.

Janny/mummer: A person who dresses in elaborate costumes and visits houses in the evenings during the holidays.

Jiggs dinner: A traditional meal usually consisting of turkey, chicken, roast beef or salt beef, served with potatoes, carrots, turnip, cabbage or greens that are all boiled in the same pot. Lots of gravy is requisite, as are yellow split peas for making peas pudding.

Jumper: Any sea animal, such as the northern pilot whale, dolphins, porpoise and tuna, that leaps out of the water and occasionally swims alongside ships.

Killick: A long stone wrapped in pliable sticks used as an anchor for fishing nets and small boats. Also, pregnant women are sometimes said to "have a rock in their killick."

Kitchen party: The inevitable end to many parties, where everyone ends up in the kitchen spacious enough to step to a tune, warm up near the stove, and drink the night away.

Labrador tea: A low-growing evergreen.

Livyer: Permanent settlers as opposed to migratory fisherman.

Logy: Heavy or fat, slow-moving or sluggish. The term can be applied to people, animals, the weather and even ships and vehicles that are overloaded.

Lumpfish: A kind of a fish, round and black, which frequently used to get caught in cod traps. 'Ugly as a lump' is an insult. This fishery is lucrative; lumpfish are harvested primarily for its caviar.

Missus: Colloquial nickname for any female whose name is unknown or forgotten, used especially when relating a tale about her (as in 'Buddy' for a male). Also used when men refer to their wives, as in "then the missus told me to get off me lazy arse."

Outport: An isolated coastal settlement where people grow up with strong cultural traditions.

Take 5 MARK CALLANAN'S TOP FIVE
NEWFINESE WORDS

Mark Callanan was born and raised in St. John's. *Scarecrow*, his first collection of poetry, was published by Killick Press in 2003. Mark reviews books for *Newfoundland Quarterly*, *The Independent*, *Atlantic Books Today* and *Books in Canada*.

1. **Chummy:** The most democratic of pronouns; it can apply to an unnamed person or to any object the name of which cannot currently be recalled. As in: Pass the chummy there. This chummy? No, the other one.

2. **Cracky:** "A small, noisy mongrel dog" (DNE) bred for the sole purpose of driving the neighbourhood up the wall. Often to be heard yapping at nothing in particular. See also: strychnine, possible uses for.

3. **Dout:** Contraction of do and out; to extinguish flames or turn off a light. As in: Did you dout the lights? Yes. Did you dout the candles? Yesss! Are you going to dout that frigging cigarette? I'll dout you in a minute! I highly doubt it.

4. **Foss:** A kick. As in: Either you stop that cracky's racket or I'll give you both a foss in the arse!

5. **Screedless:** "Without a stitch of clothing" (DNE), figuratively speaking. Used in the sense of having fallen on hard times. As in: I lost my job, my wife and my self-respect. I'm screedless. If I only had a chummy I'd end it all.

DNE: Dictionary of Newfoundland English.

Partridgeberry: This plant lies low to the ground and boasts small, tart berries.

Punt: A round bottomed and keeled boat. Measuring up to 8 metres, it is guided by oars, sail or engine.

Queer hand or queer stick: An unusual person, guided by his or her own humorous and quirky character.

Quintal/Kintal: A unit of measurement equal to 112 pounds, it was once used by merchants to weigh a fisherman's production of saltfish and tally its worth in goods and supplies.

Rag-moll: A ragged beggar or a woman who is unkempt. More generally, the term can apply to a slovenly, untidy person.

Shareman: A member of a fishing crew who receives a share of the profits earned by the voyage.

Sinker or Sunker: A hazardous rock with the potential to 'sink' seafaring vessels.

Slawmeen: A dirty, unkempt person whose body, clothes and home are often untidy and/or filthy.

Sleeveen/sleiveen: A schemer, trickster, mean person or thief.

Sook/Sooky: A call to a cow, or a crybaby, as in "Don't be such a sook."

Streel: A dirty, messy and/or untidy person, especially a woman (see rag-moll).

Sulky: A two-wheeled carriage.

Swile: Another word for any North Atlantic seal.

Touton/Toutin: A flapjack or a kind of cake made with bread dough, usually fried in fat and served with butter, molasses or maple syrup.

Townie: Word describing a resident of St. John's by anyone who lives outside it.

Tuckamore: A short, wind-stunted evergreen with spreading, gnarled roots that covers the ground in a mat of green. It also describes all low stunted scrub.

Twacking: Going beyond window shopping, walking around and looking at goods, inquiring as to the prices and other information but buying nothing.

Vamps: Similar to cloth-like slippers, these are short, thick socks worn in boots to avoid chafing.

Yaffle: A handful or an armful of something that needs to be carried such as saltfish or firewood.

Yes b'y: The contraction of "yes, boy." An expression of agreement to something said, whether a statement or a question.

Youngster: A descriptor of a child or a young inexperienced "green" man who was brought to Newfoundland and Labrador for a couple of summers and winters to be educated in the ways of the fishery.

Weblinks

Dictionary of Newfoundland English Online
www.heritage.nf.ca/dictionary/d7ction.html
The definitive collection of Newfoundland and Labrador English.

The Natural World

At almost 406,000 km^2, the province of Newfoundland and Labrador covers three times as much territory as Nova Scotia, New Brunswick and Prince Edward Island combined. However, with just four percent of Canada's land mass, Newfoundland and Labrador is smaller than any of the other provinces. Still, the province's land mass is not to be sneezed at — it's larger than Japan, almost twice the size of North and South Korea combined, and is half the size of New Zealand. If it were an American state, Newfoundland and Labrador would come in fourth behind Alaska, Texas and California. The Newfoundland half of the province — with an area of 111,390 km^2 — ranks as the 15th largest island in the world.

Did you know...

that the highest peaks of Newfoundland and Labrador are all found in the Torngat Mountain range that borders the province of Quebec? The highest peak reaches 1,652 m while the lowest rises to 1,204 m, about one-eighth the height of Mount Everest.

Take 5 TOP FIVE PEAKS

1. **Mount Caubvick:** 1,652 m
2. **Torngarsoak Mountain:** 1,595 m
3. **Cirque Mountain:** 1,568 m
4. **Mount Erhart:** 1,539 m
5. **Jens Haven:** 1,531 m

Source: Natural Resources Canada

LATITUDE AND LONGITUDE

Newfoundland and Labrador lies between 46 degrees and 60 degrees north latitude, and between 52 degrees and 68 degrees west longitude. The capital city of St. John's sits in the northeast quadrant of the Avalon Peninsula, at 47 degrees north latitude and 52 degrees west longitude. These coordinates place it on the same latitude as Edmundston (New Brunswick), Seattle (Washington), and Dijon (France). It's also aligned longitudinally with Umanak (Greenland), Cayenne (French Guiana), and Passo Fundo (Brazil).

PHYSICAL SETTING

- Size: 405,720 km^2
- Area of Island of Newfoundland: 111,390 km^2
- Area of Labrador: 294,330 km^2
- Length of Island of Newfoundland's coastline: 9,656 km
- Length of Labrador's coastline: 7,886 km
- Total length of coastline: 17,542 km

Source: Newfoundland and Labrador Tourism.

NATIONAL PARKS

Newfoundland and Labrador is home to two national parks — Gros Morne and Terra Nova, both on the Island — and one new national park reserve in Labrador called Torngat Mountains.

- Total area of Gros Morne National Park: 1,942.5 km^2

THE FIVE MOST COMMON
SPECIES OF TREES IN NEWFOUNDLAND AND LABRADOR

1. Balsam fir
2. Black spruce
3. White spruce
4. White birch
5. Trembling aspen

Sources: Newfoundland and Labrador, Forest Resources; NL Department of Natural Resources.

- Total area of Terra Nova National Park: 399.9 km^2
- Total area of Torngat Mountains National Park Reserve: approximately 9,600 km^2

Sources: Atlas of Canada, Parks Canada.

SEEING THE TREES FOR THE FOREST

When European settlers came to Newfoundland they found much of it covered by extraordinarily dense, mixed forests. Today, nearly 60 percent of the province's forest — about 23 million acres — is productive and non-productive woods. Softwood accounts for 93 percent of the forest, and hardwood just 7 percent. With the Crown controlling about 95 percent of the land, it's no surprise that 98 percent of the province's forest is in government hands.

TREE GROWING

- Percentage of Newfoundland and Labrador forest that is harvested commercially each year: less than 0.5 (20,000 hectares)
- Approximate percentage of harvested areas that grow back naturally: 80
- Percentage that is reforested using seedlings, planted by hand: 20

Source: Department of Natural Resources.

MOTHER NATURE'S PRUNING

Over the past ten years, an average of 173 forest fires have burned each year in Newfoundland and Labrador. Lightning causes fewer fires here than in western parts of the country. The 2007 forest fire season saw fewer fires than average and fewer hectares burned. That year, 87 fires (only 11 caused by lightning and the rest by human-related activities)

Take 5 DR. PETER SCOTT'S TOP FIVE
RUGGED NEWFOUNDLAND AND LABRADOR PLANTS

Peter J. Scott, Ph.D., is curator of the Agnes Marion Ayre Herbarium, Department of Biology, Memorial University of Newfoundland. His research interests include the flora of the province of Newfoundland and Labrador, plant ecology, and biotechnology. He holds Canadian and U.S. patents for peat processing and he appears regularly on radio and television as a gardening columnist.

1. **Mountain alder (*Alnus crispa*) and Speckled alder (*Alnus rugosa*):** The alder has a fungus associated with its roots that captures nitrogen. This allows the alder to be the first colonizer of barren, gravel spots and to grow in very poor soil.

2. **Sheep laurel (*Kalmia angustifolia*):** This shrub is systematically taking over the forests of the province. It uses chemical warfare to inhibit seedlings of other species.

3. **Crowberry (*Empetrum nigrum*):** The crowberry forms carpets on windswept headlands, banks, and the forest floor. It can withstand winds, salt, and the trampling of many feet.

4. **Fireweed (*Epilobium angustifolium*):** Single, thin stalks dot the forest floor and seeds rest in the soil until an area is cleared of vegetation by fire or cutting. Fireweed then springs to life and takes over.

5. **Black spruce (*Picea mariana*) and white spruce (*Picea glauca*):** Spruce blanket huge areas of the province. They grow in sheltered valleys, swampy ground and bogs, and on wind-swept cliffs.

claimed 10,891.8 hectares of woodland — 4.3 productive and 10,887.5 non-productive. No lives were lost in forest fires in the province during 2007. The year 1999 was the worst fire season for Newfoundland and Labrador; more than 39,291 hectares burned, claiming nearly 3,300 hectares of productive forest.

Source: Natural Resources Newfoundland and Labrador.

FARM COUNTRY

With 57 percent of the province covered in woodland and another 30 percent or so covered in fresh water, bogs, barren rock and soil, and jagged coastline, it's no wonder that only 11,000 hectares — fewer than half of one percent of the province's area — are being used for agriculture.

Early settlers and fishers often planted their own gardens or managed modest subsistence farms. In later years, commercial farming took root on the Avalon Peninsula, in parts of Bonavista, as well as in Notre Dame Bay, Trinity Bay, and in areas near the southwest coast of the Island. Starting in 1813, the arrival of skilled Irish farmers boosted Newfoundland and Labrador's agricultural output; they grew crops to feed a growing population.

By the early 1900s, agriculture was flourishing as much as it could in the colony. More than 120,000 horses, cattle and sheep grazed and some thickly wooded lands had been cleared. Confederation led to greater cultivation as the new province took advantage of federal programs to clear more land and bolster egg and hog production. In recent years, residential development has put pressure on some traditional farmland areas, especially on the Avalon near St. John's.

Did you know...

that no snakes, raccoons, skunks or porcupines call the Island home?

Take 5 — THE TOP FIVE LARGEST

LAKES IN NEWFOUNDLAND AND LABRADOR (KM²)

1. **Smallwood Reservoir** (6,527)
2. **Lake Melville** (3,069)
3. **Ashuanipi Lake** (596)
4. **Grand Lake** (537)
5. **Lac Joseph** (451)

Source: Natural Resources Canada.

WATER, WATER EVERYWHERE

Nearly 6.5 percent of Newfoundland and Labrador, about 26.1 million hectares, is covered by fresh water. The Smallwood Reservoir in Labrador, formed by the 1966 damming of the Churchill River, is the province's largest lake. The reservoir is one of the largest in the world and is the tenth largest body of fresh water in Canada.

ST. JOHN'S HARBOUR

St. John's Harbour's close proximity to the province's historic fishing grounds and its status as the easternmost port in Canada have made it Newfoundland and Labrador's major industrial port. Sadly, the harbour

Did you know...

that 75 percent of all moose-vehicle collisions happen between dusk and dawn, and 70 percent happen between June 1 and October 31?

Did you know...

that Gros Morne National Park was made a UNESCO World Heritage site in 1987?

is one of Canada's dirtiest because millions of litres of untreated sewage are pumped in each day. Not for much longer, however: a nearly $100 million project—to be completed by 2009—will provide collector sewers, a huge treatment facility, and eventually a cleaner harbour.

Source: City of St. John's.

Take 5 BRENDA MCCLELLAN'S TOP FIVE
BEST BEACHES

Brenda McClellan is a visual artist, whose work is strongly influenced by the landscape and culture of Newfoundland and Labrador. Here she gives up her take on the best beaches in Newfoundland and Labrador.

1. **The Beaches at Burgeo:** Mile after mile of amazing sandy beaches, both small and large, intersected by rocky outcrops. These are wide, shallow beaches where the water warms — they provide the best saltwater beaches for swimming. The endangered Piping Plover also nests here.

2. **The long sandy beaches on the Gulf of St. Lawrence, north of Gros Morne National Park:** I have found the best driftwood sculptures along these beaches.

3. **The wide rocky beach at St. Vincent's on the southern Avalon:** This beach has a sudden drop-off allowing whales to come close to shore in the early summer. It is a great beach from which to watch diving gannets.

4. **"Porcupine Strand" in Labrador, 10 miles north of Cartwright:** This amazing sandy beach is 56 km long and was known as "Wonderstrand" by the Vikings.

5. **The thousands of small secretive beaches along 11,000 miles of coastline:** These are accessible by boat, sometimes appearing suddenly along coastal hiking trails.

Take 5 FIVE WILDLIFE SPECIES AT RISK

1. **Newfoundland Pine Marten** (threatened)
2. **Piping Plover** (endangered)
3. **Polar Bear** (special concern)
4. **Wolverine** (endangered)
5. **Peregrine Falcon** (special concern)

Source: Committee on the Status of Endangered Wildlife in Canada.

CONTINENTAL SHELF AND SLOPE

The continental shelf off the coast of Newfoundland and Labrador ranges in width from 100 km to 600 km, and in depth from 50 m to 400 m. Most of the continental shelf lies within Canada's 320 km fisheries management zone.

BANKING ON IT

Shallow areas over the continental shelf are called banks. Among the most prolific fishing banks in North Atlantic are the Grand Banks, located southeast of Newfoundland. The Grand Banks cover about 282,500 km^2, with water depths between 25 and 100 m. Before the collapse of its cod stocks, the Grand Banks were some of the richest fishing grounds in the world.

Despite Canada's 1992 cod moratorium, foreign fleets fishing outside the nation's 320 km limit continue to overfish the Grand Banks — more than 500 citations have been issued to international fishers in the last 20 years. The Banks are also the site of lucrative oil fields, including Hibernia, Terra Nova and White Rose.

Did you know...

that there were no chipmunks on the island of Newfoundland before 1962?

Take 5 FIVE PLANT SPECIES AT RISK

1. **Barrens Willow** (endangered)
2. **Fernald's Milk-Vetch** (special concern)
3. **Northern Rockcress** (endangered)
4. **Boreal Felt Lichen** (special concern)
5. **Fernald's Braya** (threatened)

Source: Environment Canada.

MIGRANT MOOSE

The ubiquitous moose is not native to the Island of Newfoundland. Two were introduced in Gander Bay in 1878, four more in Howley in 1904, and since then nature has taken its productive course. Today, somewhere between 125,000 and 150,000 of the large mammals live on the Island, and this is despite the fact that each year 24,000 are taken by hunters. Moose are now so prolific they've become a nuisance on the highways and biways of Newfoundland. Each year there are about 700 collisions between moose and cars in the province, and often the cars and people involved come out the worse for it.

Sources: Parks Canada; The Rural News; Salmonier Nature Park; Dept. of Environment & Conservation.

ATLANTIC PUFFIN

The Atlantic puffin is instantly recognizable by its white face and large and colourful orange, yellow, and blue-grey bill—in which, during breeding season, it carries a dozen or more capelin back to its single chick. It's known locally as "sea parrot" or "hatchet-face" for its distinctive looks.

The province is home to North America's three largest breeding colonies. With roughly 260,000 pairs, the top nesting location is the Witless Bay islands; Baccalieu Island and the Gannet Islands in Labrador rank next.

Puffins breed in burrows or crevices in rocky cliffs. They dive from the water's surface after food, using their short wings to go as deep as 60 m in pursuit of prey. They don't take to the air as easily, however — scrambling frantically along the surface until airborne, flapping their wings at hundreds of beats per minutes in flight, and often crash-landing when out of danger.

WHO LET THE DOGS OUT?

The Newfoundland was first bred as a working dog and was traditionally used in Newfoundland and Labrador for hauling sleds and small carts loaded with firewood, fish, and fishing gear, or for carrying packs. Massively strong, with large and partially webbed feet, the dogs are well suited to marshy terrain and sandy or pebbly beaches and are excellent swimmers. Their coats are generally black, though other colours occur; they're also double-thick and water-resistant.

There are many stories about the breed's heroic rescues of shipwrecked travellers, capsized fishermen, and small children swept into the icy waters around our coasts. One of the most famous Newfoundland dogs was Gander. Named for his birthplace on the island, this World War II hero was posthumously awarded a medal for bravery for saving a group of Canadian soldiers — he picked up a live grenade and carried it away from them.

The intelligence, bravery, and sweet disposition of the Newfoundland dog make it a breed especially suited to families with children — particularly if they don't mind caring for a pet who may weigh more than any other single family member, eats an enormous amount, and whose thick, coarse coat requires ongoing maintenance.

A WILD DELICACY

Bakeapples (also known as cloudberries) are a Newfoundland delicacy whose name may come either from the French "baie qu'appelle" or from the berry's taste when ripe, which is like a baked apple. Growing only in the wild in the province's peat bogs, this member of the rose family looks like a large, yellow-orange raspberry and has a (some say acquired) honey-like taste. Much valued for use in jams and pies, the bakeapple is high in vitamin C and low in calories.

Weblinks

Wildlife at Risk

http://www.env.gov.nl.ca/env/wildlife/wildlife_at_risk.htm

This Newfoundland and Labrador government site details the character and habitat of at-risk and endangered flora and fauna in the province. It provides a link to research and reports on the status of various species.

National Parks and Historic Sites

http://www.pc.gc.ca/pn-np/nl/grosmorne/index_E.asp

This federal government website offers the historic significance of its national sites in Newfoundland and Labrador, and provides information concerning visits.

Bakeapple Recipes

http://www.tidespoint.com/food/bakeapple_recipes.shtml

Never tried bakeapples? Give the delicate-flavoured berries a shot with these recipes, available on the web courtesy of Tidespoint.com.

Weather

The weather in Newfoundland and Labrador is as varied as the people who live here; no two days — make that two hours — are the same. The province's proximity to the ocean is a major influence on the climate, keeping winter air temperatures marginally warmer along the coasts, while summer temperatures are cooler. The province's weather includes abundant precipitation and cloud, with lesser amounts of sunshine, humidity and strong, persistent winds… not to mention a wee bit of fog.

AVERAGE TEMPERATURES (°C)
St. John's

Jan	Feb	Mar	Apr	May	Jun	Jul	Aug	Sep	Oct	Nov	Dec
-4.8	-5.4	-2.5	1.6	6.2	10.9	15.4	15.5	11.8	6.9	2.6	-2.2

Happy Valley-Goose Bay

Jan	Feb	Mar	Apr	May	Jun	Jul	Aug	Sep	Oct	Nov	Dec
-18.1	-16.3	-9.6	-1.7	5.1	11	15.4	14.5	9.2	2.4	-4.5	-13.9

AND THE WINNER IS . . .
• Record high temperature in Newfoundland: 36.7°C, Botwood, 1976

They Said It

> "There are two seasons in Newfoundland: winter and bad ice fishing."
> —**Traditional Newfoundland saying.**

- Record high temperature in Labrador: 37.8 °C, at Goose Bay, July 4, 1944
- Record low temperature in Newfoundland: -41.1 °C, at Woodale Bishop's Falls (1975)
- Record low temperature in Labrador: -54°C, at Labrador City
- Record daily rainfall: 127 mm in St. John's, Sept. 19, 2001
- Record daily snowfall: 68.4 cm (St. John's, April 1999)

Source: Environment Canada.

The Sinking Of The Ocean Ranger

The stormy North Atlantic has claimed many lives. One of the deadliest storms occurred on February 15, 1982, about 315 km southeast of St. John's. On that infamous day, the Ocean Ranger offshore oilrig capsized and sank, taking the lives of all on board.

The Ocean Ranger was just six years old, and at the time the largest rig of its kind. It was thought to be unsinkable. The deadly storm that claimed the rig developed south of Newfoundland on Valentine's Day and churned its way to the Grand Banks over night. By sunset, the wind and seas were rising, the wind reaching speeds of 168 km/h and the waves heights of 30 m by evening.

A huge wave slammed into the rig at 7 pm, shattering a porthole in the ballast control room. Water flooded in, causing problems with the electrical system used to control the stability of the rig. By 1:00 am, the rig was listing dangerously. At 1:09 am, an SOS went out: "We're listing badly and we need to get the seamen off the rig." Twenty-one minutes later came the message that the crew was abandoning the rig in lifeboats. By 3:15, the Ocean Ranger had disappeared from radar.

Despite rescue efforts, all 84 crewmembers, 56 of them Newfoundlanders, were lost. Only 22 bodies were recovered. A Royal Commission assigned to investigate the disaster blamed the tragedy on design flaws and a lack of safety equipment and training.

They Said It

"The summers in Newfoundland are comparatively short. Now cool, now warm, mind and body will be benefited by the variety. The open air, in the shape of oxygen and ozone, is probably more wholesome than is found in most countries."

— **Philip Tocque, Kaleidoscope Echoes (1895) quoted in Moyles, Complaints is many and various**

SUNSHINE

- Number of sunny days, annually: 268.76
- Annual hours of sunshine in Newfoundland: 1,563
- The Canadian average: 1,925
- Average annual numbers of hours of sunshine in Canada's sunniest city, Calgary: 2,314
- Percentage of summer days that are sunny in Newfoundland: 42
- In December, the least sunny month, the daily average number of sunny hours: 2
- Number of days of smoke and haze each year: 3.42

ST. JOHN'S: WEATHER CHAMP

Of Canada's major cities, St. John's is the foggiest (124 days, beating Halifax's 122), snowiest (359 cm, next to Quebec City's 343), wettest (1,514 mm, topping Halifax's 1,491), windiest (24.3 km/h average speed, next to Regina's 20.7), and cloudiest (1,497 hours of sunshine, next to Charlottetown's 1,818 hours). The bottom line? St. John's has the third mildest winters in Canada after Victoria and Vancouver.

Did you know...

that no place on the Island of Newfoundland is more than 100 km from the sea?

BRUCE WHIFFEN'S TOP FIVE
MEMORABLE MOMENTS AS A
NEWFOUNDLAND WEATHER FORECASTER

Born, raised and educated in Bonavista, Bruce Whiffen is a meteor-ologist with Environment Canada who has spent most of his career at the Newfoundland Weather Centre in Gander. He confirms that Newfoundland is a meteorologist's paradise. In other places in North America people will say; if you don't like the weather when you look out your front window, wait ten minutes. Bruce prefers this version; "In Newfoundland, if you don't like the weather when you look out your front window, look out your back window."

1) On February 14, 1982, I was a student at Memorial University. Walking to my apartment on that bitterly cold Sunday evening, I was barely able to make my way in heavy winds and blinding snow. My parents told me the next day that they'd had the same problem in Bonavista, walking home arm-in-arm from church — I think it gave them quite a scare. Though I hadn't known it that night, out on the Grand Banks the Ocean Ranger (then the largest drill rig in the world) was already listing. It sank a few hours later, early on February 15, and all 84 crewmembers were lost. I clearly recall that in the aftermath of the storm, the sky was the deepest blue I had ever seen.

2) A few minutes into my very first shift as a forecaster at the Newfoundland Weather Centre in Gander (May 1985), the shift supervisor, who had perhaps 25 years experience throughout Canada, introduced himself to me. When he learned that I'd studied at MUN and taken the government meteorology training program in Toronto, he said, "Well you can forget all of that — you're forecasting in Newfoundland now."

3) Near the end of the night shift (around 7 am) on December 12, 1985, a call came in from the Gander International Airport tower that a plane had gone down on takeoff. As required, our observer immediately did a "check ob" for current weather conditions. The plane, an Air Arrow DC-8, had 256 on board — mostly members of the U.S Army's 101st Airborne Division returning home. Normally we're fairly chatty towards the end of a shift, but things became very quiet. I finished at 8:00, left with a colleague, and we met someone returning from the crash site. He felt no one could have survived. Passengers had been sent to nearby hospitals, but it was too late. I heard from a friend who was at the Grand Falls-Windsor hospital that when official word came that there were no survivors, many of the hospital workers cried. It was the worst aviation disaster in Canadian history at the time.

4) On Easter Monday, April 5, 1999, I was working the day shift at the Gander weather office. We'd issued a blizzard warning for the Avalon Peninsula but the storm was slower than expected. The St. John's media kept calling and asking where the blizzard was — and I kept telling them to keep the faith. Over 80 cm of snow eventually fell that day and overnight.

5) Years ago I was getting my hair cut and the barber, a real talker who didn't know me, regaled me about the lousy forecasts. Eventually, perhaps because he needed to catch his breath, he asked: "So — what do you do?"

Take 5 FIVE NEWFOUNDLAND AND LABRADOR

WEATHER WORDS

1. **Mauzy:** damp, warm, muggy weather.
2. **Logy:** oppressively humid weather.
3. **Misky:** light rain or mist.
4. **Scad:** a sudden, brief rain or snow shower.
5. **Scuddy:** conditions that are suddenly gusty.

RAIN

- Average number of rainy days per year in Newfoundland and Labrador: 196.48
- Average annual rainfall amount: 1,060.77 mm
- Percentage of precipitation that falls as rain: 75
- Amount of rain that falls annually along the south coast, the province's rainiest spot: 1,650 mm
- Greatest annual precipitation recorded in the province: 2,253 mm in 1983 at Pools Cove

GROWING SEASON

As with most provinces, the growing season in Newfoundland varies from place to place.
- Newfoundland's south coast: 150 days
- Avalon Peninsula: 125 days
- Interior: 100 days
- Labrador: 60-120 days

Did you know...

that the people of Upper Cove Island, near Conception Bay, commemorate February 3rd as Coombs's Day? On that date 200 years ago, several members of the local Coombs family perished in a snowstorm.

They Said It

"*Incest and poor diet have long been put forward to explain Newfoundland politics and Newfoundland politicians but, to my very own mind at least, not enough weight has been given to climate. It's hard to be a warm, meaningful, sincere, relevant human being when, for nine months of the year, you may step out the door on green grass in the morning and come back to supper with the snow halfway up to the window ledges.*"

— Humorist Ray Guy

SNOW
- Average annual snowfall in all of Newfoundland and Labrador: 452 cm
- In St. John's: 359 cm
- In Gander: 443 cm
- In Labrador: 480 cm
- Percentage of annual precipitation that falls as snow: 25
- On average, there are 101.85 snow days each year in Newfoundland and Labrador, making it second only to Quebec.
- Number of blowing snow days: 28.57
- Average number of days per year there is snow on the ground somewhere in the province (the fifth longest snow cover in Canada): 183.21
- The amount of snow that falls each spring in the province, making it Canada's snowiest spring: 140.5 cm

Did you know...

that scientists think that Newfoundland and Labrador has a climate that is too cold for the mosquito-borne West Nile virus?

They Said It

PASS THE SHOVEL

Cartwright, in Labrador, holds the record for the greatest recorded snowfall over five consecutive days. On January 1, 1965, 182 cm blanketed the community. The largest snowfall amount in one season occurred in the winter of 2001 with 648.4 cm falling on St. John's — which ended up costing the city a whopping $12.4 million to clean up. Most years, St. John's budgets approximately $6.6 million for snow removal.

Source: Environment Canada.

WHITE CHRISTMAS

Odds are good that wherever you live in Newfoundland and Labrador you'll have a white Christmas. If you live on the Avalon Peninsula, flip a coin; you have a 50-50 chance. If you live in St. John's, you've got a better chance with a 65 percent probability of snow on the ground December 25. Compare this to Toronto's 57 percent odds, Montreal's 80 percent, Vancouver's 11 percent, and Whitehorse's 100 percent. For the record, Goose Bay, Labrador, has never recorded a green Christmas.

The greatest snowfall ever on Christmas day in St. John's was 20.3 cm in 1955, while Goose Bay recorded 27.6 cm in 1984.

Sources: The Weather Network and Environment Canada.

Did you know...

that Daniels Harbour became the Newfoundland and Labrador town with the most lightning storms in a single day when it logged seven in a 24-hour period?

Take 5 FIVE NEWFOUNDLAND AND LABRADOR
WEATHER SAYINGS

1. Red sky at night, sailors delight; red sky at morn, sailors be warned.
2. When the wind is in the south, it blows the bait in the fish's mouth.
3. Rainbow in the east, sailor's at peace; rainbow in the west, sailor's in distress.
4. Pale moon doth rain; red moon doth blow; white moon doth neither rain nor snow.
5. May snow is good for sore eyes.

LABRADOR CHILL
• Approximate number of nights a year in which the Labrador temperature drops below -30 °C: 40

LIGHTNING STORMS
Newfoundland and Labrador holds many weather records, but lightning events make no part of them. Each year St. John's gets only seven flashes of lightning per 100 km and Goose Bay only six. Compare this to the 251 flashes seen in Windsor, Ontario, the lightning capital of Canada.

They Said It

"The rigour of the winters in Newfoundland has excited the curiosity and inquiries of many philosophical writers. Although lying on the same parallel with the most fertile parts of France, yet such is the severity of the climate, that it is not an unusual circumstance, in St. John's, to find, at the breakfast table, the tea-cup frozen to the saucer, although filled with boiling water, at the moment."

— **Edward Chapelle, British navy officer, circa 1813.**

Take 5 FIVE FOGGIEST PLACES
IN NEWFOUNDLAND AND LABRADOR
(DAYS OF FOG/YEAR)

1. **Argentia** (206)
2. **Belle Isle and Cape Race** (160)
3. **Trepassey** (158)
4. **St. Lawrence** (147)
5. **St. John's** (124)

Source: Environment Canada.

WHAT'S WITH THE WIND?

Winnipeg is known as Canada's windy city, but this claim to fame is just plain wrong. St. John's, with average wind speeds of 24.3km/h, is actually Canada's windiest city. It's not the windiest community in the province, though. That honour goes to Bonavista, where the average annual wind speed is 28 km/h.

Nationally, Newfoundland and Labrador is the third windiest province, with an average wind speed of 18.52 km/h. These breezes generally blow from the west, but this varies, particularly between inland and coastal locations. In the province as a whole, light winds occur on 211 days of the year, and the calmest community is St. Albans, in the sheltered Bay d'Espoir on Newfoundland's south coast. Average yearly wind speeds there are 11.5 km/h.

Did you know...

that in 2004 the *Canadian Oxford English Dictionary* added the word "Wreckhouse winds" to its word catalogue? The word is defined as "extremely strong winds, which blow across Cape Ray from the Long Range Mountains in Newfoundland."

WRECKHOUSE WINDS

Newfoundland and Labrador's "Wreckhouse winds" are famous. Strong southeasterly winds blowing out of valleys in western Newfoundland's Long Range Mountains sometimes create gusts of 150km/h (about the same as a category 2 hurricane) when they emerge in the Wreckhouse area, about 20 km north of Port aux Basques. When the railroads still ran, these gusts could blow trains off right off the tracks, and they can still topple transport trucks on the TransCanada highway.

Source: Newfoundland and Labrador Department of Education.

Winter Houses

The harsh Newfoundland and Labrador climate has profoundly influenced its people and society. An interesting example is "winter housing," an old pattern of seasonal migration that in some places characterized outport life into the 20th century.

Newfoundlanders and Labradorians living in isolated coastal outports were well-attuned to the region's weather. During milder spring and summer months, outport fishers lived along the coast. When cold winds blew and ice clogged harbours, they and their families moved inland seeking shelter from the harsh winters.

They resumed life in their "winter houses" or "tilts," which were temporary and cheaply constructed homes heated with fireplaces vented though a hole cut in the roof. Their winter houses offered access to inland game (a welcome change of diet) and ready access to wood, much needed for fuel and for repairing fishing equipment.

As the coastal population grew and as communities were modernized, the practice of winterhousing declined. This important cultural practice lives on, however, in the names of towns such as Winterhouse, and Winterhouse Brook.

HURRICANES

The hurricanes that reach Newfoundland and Labrador — or "extra-tropical systems," as they are called when they begin to weaken — have been increasing in number and intensity in recent years. Some meteorologists think this is because the ocean waters off the province's shores are gradually getting less frigid — part of the complex of trends known as global warming.

The warmer the water underneath the storm, the more energy it picks up, and the stronger the winds and punch it will pack. For those who might wish to get close to the action, August, September, and October are the months most likely to bring hurricane activities to Newfoundland and Labrador.

Take 5 — TOP 5 MOST DESTRUCTIVE HURRICANES IN NEWFOUNDLAND AND LABRADOR HISTORY

1. **"The Independence Hurricane," September 1775:** This ferocious storm killed 4,000 sailors, mostly British, and is the sixth deadliest hurricane of all time in the North Atlantic.
2. **Hurricane Gabrielle, September 19, 2001:** This storm buffeted the Avalon Peninsula with wind and rain; in 10 hours, more than 160 mm of rain swamped Cape Race. In St. John's, 127 mm fell in six hours, the most to ever fall on the capital in a single day.
3. **Hurricane Luis, September 11, 1995:** Luis killed 16 people and cost a half billion dollars when he struck the Avalon Peninsula dumping 100 mm of rain and bringing winds of 70 knots.
4. **Hurricane Ella, September 5, 1978:** As Ella passed south of Newfoundland she brought wind speeds exceeding 220 km/h. In St. John's, the storm dumped 45 mm of rain whipped by 115 km/h winds.
5. **Hurricane Michael, October 20, 2000:** As Michael hit Newfoundland, he registered winds of 160 km/h. The storm quickly became extra-tropical and did only light damage.

Source: Environment Canada.

They Said It

"The noise of smashing timbers, the roar of the sea, the movement of thousands of tons of rocks and beach gravel, the screams of horrified people, all blended into one indescribable crescendo."
— **Witness Paul Antle's description of the November 1929 tsunami that devastated the Burin Peninsula, from Paul O'Neill's** *Breakers: Stories from Newfoundland and Labrador.*

NOT IN KANSAS, TOTO

Although well known for its persistent high winds, Newfoundland and Labrador rarely experiences tornadoes. However a number of these dangerous storms have been confirmed in the province, and others have probably gone unrecorded.

On August 16, 1997, at 8:07 pm, a tornado touched down on Main Street, Bishop's Falls, where it travelled about 150 m before returning to the thunderclouds. No one was injured, but astonished witnesses watched the funnel uproot trees and fences, scattering debris along the way.

FOG

Fog and Newfoundland and Labrador go together like codfish and scrunchins. In Newfoundland's case, fog is most often generated when warm humid air moves horizontally over the cold Atlantic Ocean. It can, and often does, engulf the coastline. Each year the entire island of Newfoundland is enshrouded in fog for 25 days, with coastal regions reporting more frequent fog.

- St. John's is the foggiest city in Canada with 124 fog days each year.
- Argentia, a community on the Avalon, is the foggiest place in the province with fog 206 days a year.
- The Labrador Straits boast 65 foggy days a year but on the whole, Labrador contends with just 30 days of fog each year. Inland gets off even easier — it records just ten foggy days annually.

Source: Environment Canada.

They Said It

SILVER THAW

Freezing rainstorms, known as a "silver thaw," can cause devastating damage and bring traffic to a standstill. On average, the province suffers through 15.93 days of freezing rain or drizzle a year, second only to Prince Edward Island. Although March is the worst month for freezing rain, it was in April 1984 that one of the worst ice storms on record paralyzed the Avalon peninsula. For three days, starting on the 11th, a coating of ice 15 cm thick accumulated on trees, overhead wires, and everything else. More than 200,000 residents were left shivering in the dark for days.

THE BIG ONE

Earthquakes are rare in the province; since 1954, only 21 small quakes have been recorded, and just one — on November 18, 1929 — has caused the province major damage. This earthquake, which measured

Did you know...

that icebergs, which "calve" (or sheer off) from glaciers, are made of compressed snow? They are fresh — not salt — water.

Did you know...

that according to SOS Canada, the largest wave recorded anywhere in the world was in Newfoundland and Labrador waters? The record-setting 30 m wave was generated by Hurricane Luis in 1995 and slammed against the luxury liner *Queen Elizabeth II* as it sailed off the south coast of Newfoundland.

7.2 on the Richter scale, had its epicenter under the sea on the Laurentian Slope and was felt throughout Atlantic Canada and as far away as Ottawa and the state of Delaware.

The shaking itself did little damage, but the same cannot be said of the tsunami it spawned. The giant tidal wave crashed into the Burin Peninsula on the south coast of Newfoundland, destroying 500 homes in 50 outports. It killed 36 people and sank 100 fishing boats. The event took an economic toll as well — more than 127,000 kilograms of salt cod valued at $23,000 was lost.

SHEILA'S BRUSH

"Sheila's Brush" is the name given to a fierce winter storm that strikes around St. Patrick's Day. Also known as "Paddy's Scad," this storm is often said to mark the end of winter. Incidentally, no one is exactly sure who "Sheila" is. It has been suggested that she was one of the first European settlers in Newfoundland, Sheila NaGiera, but legend also says she was the wife, sister or mother of St. Patrick.

Did you know...

that the International Ice Patrol (IIP) was created in 1912 after the *Titanic* collided with a North Atlantic iceberg? This organization compiles charts and broadcasts ice bulletins to warn sailors of conditions; it is financed by 17 nations around the world.

They Said It

"People were outdoors, hollering to everybody else. ...Then when we saw the water coming, everybody started to run, because it wasn't like it was coming in through the cove. It was like it was coming from the sky."

— Witness Mary McKenna's recollection of the 1929 Tsunami at Lord's Cove.

"We didn't get anything out. I got me my husband, my two kids, and my cat. That was it."

— Karen Loder, homeowner in flood and ice ravaged Badger, explaining her family's narrow escape from the deluge.

ICE, ICE EVERYWHERE

In February 2003, the small town of Badger, Newfoundland, endured an environmental double whammy. The town faced massive flooding when water levels rose 2.5 m in just one hour, prompting evacuation. Just when it seemed things could not get worse, a cold snap followed and the flooded town was entombed in 1.3 million tonnes of ice. Homes, cars, and business were all destroyed by the crush of ice.

BERGS

An iceberg is an awe-inspiring sight. Although ice conditions vary, approximately 250 icebergs per year make the 1,600 km journey from Greenland to the coasts of Newfoundland and Labrador, following the Labrador Current southward. Recent numbers of bergs off Newfoundland have ranged from none at all in 1966 to 2,202 in 1984.

In early January, when pack ice enters the Strait of Belle Isle, navigation of these waters becomes extremely hazardous. Pack ice and icebergs also drift southeastward to Notre Dame Bay, Cape Freels, and sometimes well beyond. By March, the ice reaches its southernmost point, accumulating in bays and harbours along Newfoundland's northeast coast. By April, the pack begins to recede; the icebergs carry on south with the current, and gradually melt away.

Did you know...

that on January 20, 1977, barometers in St. Anthony recorded the lowest sea-level pressure ever in Canada? The reading was 94.02 kPa.

- 88 percent of an iceberg is hidden below water
- Average speed an iceberg travels at: 0.7 km/h
- Average weight of a large iceberg: 100,000 to 200,000 tonnes
- Age of ice comprising an iceberg: as old as 15,000 years

Sources: Environment Canada; Canadian Geographic, Icebergs of Newfoundland and Labrador.

STRANDED

Three words bring joy to children like no others: "School is cancelled."
A February 2003 snowstorm on the Northern Peninsula, however, had
different results. The textbook storm, featuring 90 km/h winds, heavy
snow and whiteout conditions, started after 200 children in the town
of St. Anthony arrived at school. Unable to get home, the young
scholars were stranded at school for two nights.

Weblinks

Highway Driving Conditions
http://www.roads.gov.nl.ca/cameras/
See for yourself! View driving conditions in real time.

Environment Canada, Provincial Forecast
http://www.weatheroffice.ec.gc.ca/forecast/canada/index_e.html?id=NF
Plan your day with the Environment Canada forecast for
Newfoundland and Labrador.

Canadian Ice Service
http://ice-glaces.ec.gc.ca/App/WsvPageDsp.cfm
Updated daily, this is Canada's leading source of ice information.

Crime and Punishment

CRIME LINE

1582: The first record of piracy occurs in the waters off Newfoundland.

1729: First naval governor and justices of the peace are appointed.

1732: First town police department is established.

1750: Murder trials first held in Newfoundland.

1754: On October 11, Eleanor Power is hanged for murder, the first woman in British North America to suffer this fate. Three of her male co-conspirators were also executed.

1769: It becomes a capital crime to murder a Beothuk.

1792: A supreme court for civil and criminal cases is established.

1835: The last public hanging is held — entertainment-starved St. John's residents gather at Market House Hill to watch John Flood be executed for highway robbery.

1917: On January 1, Prohibition is enacted.

1925: Prohibition is rescinded.

1933: Louise Saunders, Newfoundland and Labrador's first female lawyer is called to the bar.

Escapades of Peter Easton

Even before John Guy established Newfoundland's first settlement at Cupid's in 1610, the notorious "Pirate Admiral" Peter Easton was plying the waters with as many as 40 ships and 5,000 pirate sailors.

Easton was sent to Newfoundland in 1602, a loyal privateer serving Queen Elizabeth in charge of protecting the fishing fleet. With the accession of King James I to the throne and the more peaceful international relations that followed, privateers' letters of commission were cancelled, and some of them, including Easton, turned to piracy to make a living.

Peter Easton knew the Atlantic intimately, and he practised his new "profession" with zeal, from the Caribbean to Newfoundland and the Azores. In Newfoundland he plundered harbours and ships, confiscating treasure and pressing sailors into his service. He once captured 30 ships in St. John's Harbour in one raid, taking men, money, and the English sheriff sent to bring him to justice. He was rumoured to have captured great fortunes from the Spanish in the Caribbean.

By 1612 his international operations were based in Harbour Grace, and he later moved them to Ferryland. From there Easton sought a pardon for his pirating ways, which James I, pleased with Easton's harassment of the French, offered him. News of it was slow to reach the pirate, however, who set off on another southern escapade in the meantime, to enhance his fortune and avoid capture. Eventually Easton retired to Villefranche, a free port for pirates, in the south of France, where he became part of the elite, married a wealthy woman and acquired the title "Marquis of Savoy."

1942: The Dominion of Newfoundland's last execution is carried out on May 22 when Herbert Spratt is hanged in St. John's for the murder of his fiancée, Josephine O'Brien.

1950: First post-Confederation murder occurs, in January.

1965: On July 15, the first post-Confederation death sentence is handed down (the federal government commutes it to life in prison along with all capital sentences in Canada).

1975: Allegations of sexual impropriety at Mount Cashel orphanage are silenced and the accused Christian Brothers shuttled to other provinces and new postings.

1981: Dana Bradley disappears on December 14 from St. John's. Her body is found four days later in woods outside the city; the 14-year-old had been bludgeoned to death. The police interview thousands of people but no one is charged. (They will continue to get about 50 tips a year.)

1989: Roman Catholic Priest James Hickey is charged with sexual molestation; this leads to investigations and several Christian Brothers at Mount Cashel are charged and sentenced to prison. A Royal Commission, the Hughes Inquiry, is struck to investigate.

1991: The Hughes Inquiry releases its report, concluding that sexual abuse at Mount Cashel had been covered up and recommending compensation for victims.

1992: The Newfoundland and Labrador branch of Crime Stoppers is founded.

1994: Gregory Parsons is sentenced to life in prison for murder, a crime he did not commit.

1996: The government of Newfoundland and Labrador pays $11.5 million to the victims of Mount Cashel.

1998: Gregory Parsons is acquitted on all charges.

2002: Gregory Parsons is awarded damages on humanitarian grounds.

Take 5 FIVE PIRATES WITH NEWFOUNDLAND LINKS

1. **Peter Easton:** His skill on the water was unmatched; his decades-long reputation as a "notorious pirate" extended to England and beyond. In the early 1600s, Easton based himself in Newfoundland, plundered its coasts, and worried French, Spanish, and Basque ships on the high seas.

2. **Henry Mainwaring:** This charming master mariner was sent to Newfoundland to arrest Easton. Upon arriving in Newfoundland, he fell in love with pirating and took up the business himself, assuming Easton's place when he retired.

3. **John Nutt:** Nutt patrolled the waters off Newfoundland from 1620 to 1623 and had the distinction of being on the Crown's blacklist. After his relatively short career, he requested and received a pardon. When he returned home, he was nonetheless imprisoned and sentenced to hang. Friends in high places managed to secure him a last-minute pardon.

4. **Marquis de la Rade:** This French pirate, along with his 400 men, wrought havoc on the shores of Newfoundland in the early 17th century. In 1628, he and his men attacked and pillaged English settlers at Trinity and Conception Bay.

5. **Edward Low:** Even his pirate friends were shocked by Low's brutality. He was especially fond of torturing victims, forcing them to eat their own amputated lips or ears. His cruelty was visited upon the whole of the Atlantic, and Newfoundland did not escape. He was eventually executed for his crimes.

2003: Government announces a public inquiry into how justice is carried out in the province, to be headed by retired Chief Justice of Canada, Antonio Lamer.

2005: Parsons is awarded an additional $650,000 bringing his total compensation to $1.3 million.

2006: Lamer Inquiry Report is released. The inquiry focused on the wrongful convictions of Parsons and Randy Druken, and an 8-year delay in hearing Ronald Dalton's appeal; the Report includes 45 recommendations for improving the administration of justice.

2006: A break in the unsolved 1993 disappearance of Dale Worthman and Kimberley Lockyer occurs when police discover their bodies on a woods road outside St. John's (allegedly following a tip from a psychic). Joseph (Joey) Anthony Oliver is arrested January 15, 2007, and police say there are additional suspects. He is released on bail in January 2008 — a decision that is later appealed.

2007: An emotionally troubled Nelson Hart is convicted of first-degree murder in the 2002 drowning of his twin 3-year-old daughters. The conviction is partly enabled by an elaborate sting operation, during which the RCMP involve Hart in a fake crime ring.

2008: Dr. Sean Buckingham is sentenced to 7 years for sexual assault and drug trafficking bringing to a close a sensational trial in which drug-addicted women testified the St. John's doctor traded narcotics for sexual acts.

Did you know...

that between 1750 and 1791 there were 20 trials for murder in Newfoundland?

I Killed My Girl

Newfoundland hanged its last criminal in December 1942. A tale of love, betrayal and tragedy, the murder of Josephine O'Brien and the trial of her fiancé Herbert Spratt horrified Newfoundlanders, many of whom sympathized with the young accused.

On the evening of March 17, 1942, St. Patrick's Day, 22-year-old Herbert and his young fiancée, 20-year-old Josephine, were relaxing in the home of Spratt's brother. Just three months from their June wedding, the couple was happily discussing their wedding and married life when Josephine made a startling admission; she believed she was pregnant.

Herbert, who would later declare that he "never had anything to do with a girl in my life," knew he was not the baby's father. He flew into a mad rage. Grabbing an iron, he bludgeoned Josephine to death and fled. Aghast at what he had done, he told his family and friends, "I did something awful; I killed my girl."

Josephine's body was discovered by midnight, and the investigation quickly led police to Herbert. He immediately confessed his crime. Spratt's defence argued that his actions were the result of a weakened mental and emotional state. Spratt had recently been relieved of duty in the navy on medical grounds — he had tuberculosis. But there was more to the story; his military discharge did not come before he saw active battle in World War II. Just a year before the murder, Spratt and his crewmates narrowly survived a sea battle with the notorious German battleship *Bismarck*. This experience, Spratt's defence argued, left him prone to emotional and uncontrollable outbursts.

The defence won sympathy, but no amount of sympathy could save his life. After just one day of testimony and 35 minutes of jury deliberation, Spratt was sentenced to be "hanged by the neck until dead." An appeal failed. Spratt spent his final days lamenting what he had done to Josephine — a girl who, coroners later testified, had not been pregnant after all. At 8 am on May 8, Spratt made the long walk to the gallows in the penitentiary courtyard.

CRIME BY THE NUMBERS

Newfoundland and Labrador records a rate of 6,054.8 criminal code incidents per 100,000 people, which puts it in 11th place among all Canadian provinces. The Northwest Territories records the highest rate of criminal code incidents with 41,468.2, while Ontario records the lowest with 5,689.2. Canada as a whole records 7,518.5.

Source: Statistics Canada.

CRIME ON THE ROCK (PER 100,000):

- 1.4 homicides
- 733.8 assaults
- 23.4 robberies involving violence
- 130.7 motor vehicle thefts
- 14.7 other thefts over $5,000
- 1,251.8 thefts under $5,000
- 736 break-and-enters
- 67.1 sexual assaults
- 220.7 cases of impaired driving

Source: Statistics Canada.

They Said It

"I bought a locket for my girl for Easter. I paid $8.50 for it and I never gave it to her yet. I love my girl; I loved her. She said she was going to have a baby, I don't know if I killed her at six o'clock yesterday or the day before. What did I do it for?"

— **Herbert Spratt's admission to his parents.**

TO SERVE AND PROTECT (2007)

- Number of police officers in Newfoundland and Labrador: 838
- Number in Canada: 64,134
- Number per 100,000 citizens in Newfoundland and Labrador: 165.4
- Officers per 100,000 citizens in Canada: 195.2

Source: Statistics Canada.

Take 5 JACK FITZGERALD'S FIVE

MOST INTRIGUING CRIMES IN NEWFOUNDLAND AND LABRADOR

Jack Fitzgerald was born and educated in St. John's. During his career he has been a journalist, a feature writer, editor, political columnist, reporter and public affairs writer. During the last years of the Smallwood administration, he was assistant director of Public Relations with the Government of Newfoundland and Labrador. Fitzgerald also hosted a regular radio program featuring off-beat Newfoundland stories on radio station VOFM. In addition to writing about unusual happenings relating to Newfoundland and Newfoundlanders, Fitzgerald has authored a series of Newfoundland crime-and-punishment stories and historical pieces.

1. **The Chinese murders on Carters Hill in St. John's:** In 1922, three Chinese laundrymen, Hong Lee, Hong King Hig, and So Ho King, were murdered by a fourth, Wo Fen Game, with whom they had a quarrel. At the trial the only motive that emerged was the killer's distress at earning far less than he had been promised.

2. **The deaths of 99 people in the Knights of Columbus fire in St. John's:** The events of the tragic evening of December 12, 1942, were broadcast live over the radio station VOCM as they happened. That night, 350 revellers, mostly servicemen, had assembled at the popular watering hole. Because it was wartime and blackouts were in place, doors were locked and windows barricaded, which prevented people from escaping. Horrified Newfoundlanders listened as their radios relayed the screams of victims trapped in the inferno. Although no one was charged for

IN THE LINE OF DUTY

1861: Cst. Jeremiah Dunn; hit by a stone thrown by rioters.

1870: Chief Cst. Charles Calpin; accidental gun discharge.

1884: Sergeant Thomas Fennessey; accidentally smothered in snow bank.

1936: Ranger Danny Corcoran; tetanus resulting from being lost for almost a month in a harsh climate.

1939: Corporal Michael Greene; along with his horse, fell through ice.

setting the fire, some have suggested it was an act of arson, even of Nazi sabotage.

3. **The murder of Constable William Moss:** During a heated labour dispute in Badger — later known as the Badger Riot — the officer was struck in the head with a board and died two days later of his injuries.

4. **The murder of Constable Robert Amey:** Amey was 24 years old when four men broke out of Her Majesty's Penitentiary in St. John's. The men stole a car and headed west. Near Whitbourne they hit a roadblock set up by Amey and another officer and got out of the car. The escaped inmates rushed the other officer, taking his revolver and shooting Amey. The other officer managed to secure Amey's gun and arrest all four escapees.

5. **The abuse of young boys by the Christian Brothers of Mount Cashel Orphanage:** Hundreds of orphaned boys were sexually and physically abused by the Christian Brothers in charge of their care. Victims, many of whom suffered long-term mental-health issues as a result of the abuse, sued their former caretakers. The lawsuit led to a Royal Commission that uncovered the horrors of their childhoods. Nine Christian Brothers were convicted and sentenced to prison terms ranging from one to thirteen years. In 1990, the orphanage was closed (and subsequently demolished), and two years later an official apology was made to the victims.

1946: Ranger Michael Collins; on-duty motorcycle accident.

1954: Cst. Francis Stamp; heart attack.

1958: Cst. Terry Hoey; shot while responding to a domestic dispute.

1959: Cst. William Moss; struck with a board by rioters.

1964: Cst. Robert Amey; shot by escaped inmates while attempting to arrest them.

Source: NL Police and Peace Officers' Memorial Association.

MURDEROUS DUO

If pirating could be said to be a business, there were no better entrepreneurs than the pirate couple Eric and Maria Cobham. From 1740 to 1760, they sank every ship they plundered in the Gulf of St. Lawrence. Eric had a reputation for brutality, but he was outdone by his wife.

Maria had a penchant for mutilating her victims or, if she had time to kill, dining with them while she watched them writhe and die from the poison with which she had laced their food. Eventually she went insane, and the last life she took was her own, perhaps with the help of poison from her doting husband, and most certainly with the help of a very tall Newfoundland cliff.

Eric Cobham retired to France where he became a magistrate. On his deathbed he told stories of his criminal life that were published posthumously.

Did you know...

that the RCMP has 44 detachments in Newfoundland and Labrador and a force of 750 full and part-time employees? It polices 60 percent of the province's population and 82 percent of its geographical area. The Mounties took up these duties in 1949, following the province's entry into Canada. Many officers of Newfoundland's existing forces — the Newfoundland Rangers and the Royal Newfoundland Constabulary (RNC) — joined the RCMP at that time. The Newfoundland Rangers disbanded, and the RNC became the municipal force of the City of St. John's.

MOTHER OF SEVEN

In August of 1833, John Snow of Port de Grave, went missing. No body was found, but blood spatters at the wharf suggested foul play. A local barrel maker, Tobias Mandeville, and Arthur Spring, an assistant to Snow, were convicted of the man's murder.

Mandeville and Spring each claimed the other had pulled the trigger; Mandeville was in love with the victim's wife while Spring was unhappy with his wages. Their stories both implicated Snow's pregnant wife, Catherine Snow, a mother of six.

Although Catherine insisted that she had not been party to her husband's death, she was charged as an accessory. Based on what prosecutors called "a chain of circumstantial evidence," they were able to link Catherine and Springer romantically and claimed Catherine had been aware of her husband's impending murder. The jury was instructed to either acquit Catherine or find her guilty.

In mere minutes, the jury determined Catherine Snow was a murderer. Many St. John's residents were outraged. Aided by local clergy, they lobbied for her sentence to be commuted. Petitions fell on deaf ears. On July 21, 1833, following the birth of her baby, Catherine Snow was hanged from gallows erected outside the courthouse.

OUTLAWING LIQUOR

The turn of the 20th century saw Prohibition become a pressing social issue in Newfoundland (although as early as 1844 the Irish temperance movement had more than 10,000 members). In 1915, nearly 25,000 Newfoundlanders who believed booze to be a social evil or a sin (or both) voted for a total ban on alcohol. A mere 5,300 voted for the right to raise a glass of cheer. The "ayes" had it. On January 1, 1917, Prohibition became law. Except for "medicinal purposes," Newfoundlanders could not legally drink again until the law was repealed in 1925.

NAFO

The Northwest Atlantic Fisheries Organization (NAFO) is an international body established in 1979 to manage fish stocks outside Canada's 320 km limit. Currently, Canada spends $30 million annually on aerial surveillance and at-sea patrols in the fishable ground that is the NAFO Regulatory Area (NRA).

Responding to criticism of "toothlessness" and the continuing dwindling of many fish stocks, NAFO adopted stronger conservation and enforcement regulations in 2006. The number of "serious incidents" of infringements dropped dramatically in the following year. In 2007, Canadian inspectors issued 10 citations to foreign-flag vessels for illegal over-fishing and other offences — the lowest number in a decade of surveillance. The total number issued by Canadian enforcement officers between 1993 and 2007 was 365.

Source: Dept of Fisheries & Oceans.

WRONGFUL CONVICTION

Of the 30 or so wrongful convictions in recent Canadian headlines, three important cases were in Newfoundland and Labrador. The provincial government is currently reviewing its legal system after a two-year Royal Commission into the wrongful convictions of Randy Druken, Ronald Dalton and Gregory Parsons accused law enforcement officials of "tunnel vision."

Parsons was convicted of the second-degree murder of his mother in 1991, but was cleared of the murder in 1998 as a result of DNA testing. The province apologized in 1998 and compensated him. A childhood friend confessed to the murder in 2002 and is now serving a life sentence.

Druken was convicted of the 1993 murder of his girlfriend Brenda Young, based on absolutely no evidence, according to the Royal Commission. Druken served six years in prison before DNA evidence cleared him and implicated his brother, who had since died.

Dalton was convicted of killing his wife in 1988 and spent eight years in prison because of a poor defence from possibly burnt-out lawyers. He won an appeal in 2000 and was acquitted.

FAKIN' IT

In 2007, 298 counterfeit bank notes were passed in Newfoundland and Labrador, and two were seized by police — a tiny fraction of the 22,018 notes confiscated in the country that year. That compares to no bum bills passed in Nunavut and 53,329 passed in Ontario (and 14,993 seized, just over two thirds of the national total).

Source: RCMP.

Take 5 — FIVE RECENT DRUG BUSTS IN NEWFOUNDLAND AND LABRADOR

1. **Operation Beauford, November 2002:** A total of 1,224 grams of cocaine, 158 ecstasy pills, 306 grams of hashish, 1,814 grams of marijuana and nearly $70,000 in cash was seized.

2. **Operation Batman, February 2003:** Heading to St. John's and Happy Valley-Goose Bay when intercepted was more than $3 million in marijuana and assets worth more than $50,000.

3. **Operation Babble, September 2003:** This, the largest cash seizure in the province's history, netted $750,000 for the RCMP Proceeds of Crime Unit and about 23 kilograms of hashish.

4. **Operation Bullwinkle, June 2004:** More than 250 kilograms of marijuana, 624 grams of cocaine, 113 grams of cannabis resin oil, ten vials of steroids, 50,000 ecstasy pills, 600 prescription pills, 11 swanky autos and about $300,000 in cash were confiscated.

5. **June 2005:** This one has no catchy name, but about six tonnes of hashish was seized from a Canadian boat off the northeast coast.

Source: RCMP

Take 5 TOP FIVE CRIMES
IN NEWFOUNDLAND AND LABRADOR (2006)

1. **Theft** (604 cases / 512 guilty)
2. **Impaired Driving** (559 cases / 491 guilty)
3. **Common Assaults** (529 cases / 337 guilty)
4. **Fraud** (270 cases / 223 guilty)
5. **Breaking and Entering** (251 cases / 198 guilty)

Source: Statistics Canada.

INCARCERATION

About 31 percent of the 3,787 people convicted of crimes in Newfoundland and Labrador ended up in prison, while another 9 percent were given conditional sentences. More than half of those found guilty received probation. In Canada, the same year saw 244,572 convicted, with 33.8 percent going to the Big House, 4.6 percent receiving a conditional sentence and 44.4 percent probation.

- Percentage of offenders in Newfoundland and Labrador who end up in jail: 31.4
- Average median sentence under two years: 59 days
- Percentage of offenders who get probation: 53.7

Source: Statistics Canada.

DRUG CRIME

In 2006, there were slightly fewer than 10,000 drug arrests in Canada, with 649 of them occurring in Newfoundland and Labrador. As in the days of Prohibition, the illicit substances often made their way to the province by way of the sea.

Source: Statistics Canada; RCMP.

TAKING A BITE OUT OF CRIME

Since setting up shop in the province in 1992, Crime Stoppers has helped solve 1,390 cases, arrest 1,319 people, recover $1.46 million in stolen property, and seize just shy of $3.4 million in illegal drugs. In total, $136,025 has been paid in awards for tips.

Source: Crime Stoppers.

FINE, THEN
- Parking in a no-parking zone: $20 - $180
- Speeding (10 km over): $50 - $135
- Speeding (21 - 30km over): $200 - $300
- Using a cell phone while driving on the highway: $100 - $400
- Driving without a seatbelt: $100 - $500
- Failing to produce insurance at the scene of an accident: $100 - $200

Source: Highway Traffic Act.

Weblinks

Newfoundland and Labrador Crime Rates
www40.statcan.ca/l01/cst01/legal04a.htm
Want to see how Newfoundland and Labrador's crime rates stack up? Have a look at the tables here of 2006 statistics on crime in the Atlantic Canada provinces.

Newfoundland and Labrador Department of Justice
www.justice.gov.nl.ca/just/
From a biography of the Minister, to an archive of Newfoundland and Labrador laws and a collection of justice-related news releases, this site provides a glimpse into the justice system of the province.

Crime Stoppers of Newfoundland and Labrador
www.rocktips.ca
Stay current with the unsolved crime of the week!

Culture

Many theories have been put forward to explain Newfoundland and Labrador's disproportionately large contribution to Canadian and global culture. Is it its long history? Relationship to the stormy North Atlantic? Ethnic mix? Political turmoil? Economic hardship? Whatever its genesis, Newfoundland and Labrador is home to one of the richest and most textured cultures in Canada. Folk music, passionate writing, unique food, linguistic idiosyncrasies, and high-quality crafts are all threads of the province's colourful cultural tapestry.

ARTISTS
- Number of artists in Canada: 130,100
- Number in Newfoundland and Labrador: 1,405
- Average wage of St. John's artists: $19,300
- Number of museums in Newfoundland and Labrador: 147

RECOGNITION FOR THE ARTS
In 2006-07, the Canada Council for the Arts awarded $1.8 million in grants to artists and cultural organizations in Newfoundland and Labrador, up from $1.5 million in 2005. Twenty-four individual artists saw $267,248 or 15.8 percent of the cash, approximately one-quarter of which went to writers, while 43 arts organizations scooped up the rest.

1. "CODCO"
2. "Above and Beyond"
3. "Land & Sea"
4. "Random Passage"
5. "Hatching, Matching and Dispatching"

Disciplines from performance arts to publishing—and everything in between—received funding, with the lion's share of more than $.5 million going to the theatre. Nearly 57 percent of the funding landed in St. John's, while Corner Brook and Trinity Bay garnered 12 percent and 10.7 percent, respectively, and Labrador 1.7 percent. The province received slightly less than 1.2 percent of the Council's total funding for 2006-07 and contributed 1.1 percent of the country's artists.

Canada Council for the Arts.

THAT'S AN ORDER
- Number of Newfoundlanders and Labradorians appointed to the Order of Canada: 125
- Members of the Order: 87
- Officers of the Order: 33
- Companions of the Order: 5
- Number of members in the Order for the Arts: 12

Source: Governor General of Canada, Order of Canada.

They Said It

"I was raised on homemade bread and CODCO."
— **Filmmaker Deanne Foley on growing up in St. John's.**

Take 5   FIVE MOVIES ABOUT
NEWFOUNDLAND AND LABRADOR

1. **"John and the Missus"** (1987)
2. **"Secret Nation"** (1992)
3. **"The Shipping News"** (2001)
4. **"Rare Birds"** (2001)
5. **"Young Triffie"** (2006)

MOVIES

- Number of movie theatres: 20
- Average annual household spending on movie rentals: $84
- Average household spending on movie theatres: $71

Sources: Cansim, Empire Theatres.

THE FILM INDUSTRY

- Number of films made in 2006/07: 5 (5 documentaries and docu-dramas, 0 feature films)
- Number of TV shows made in 2006/07: 9
- Production activity for 2006/7: $2.8 million (down from $25.6 million 2005/6, and $9.2 million in 2004/5)

Source: Newfoundland and Labrador Film Development Corporation.

Take 5   FIVE CELEBRITIES
FROM NEWFOUNDLAND AND LABRADOR

1. **Gordon Pinsent**, actor
2. **Mary Walsh**, actor and comedienne
3. **Seamus O'Regan**, host of Canada A.M.
4. **Rick Mercer**, comedian
5. **Rex Murphy**, CBC host, *Globe and Mail* columnist and author

LIVE THEATRE

- Number of theatre companies: 6
- Number of people who attend live theatre each year: 96,515

Source: Statistics Canada.

LITERATURE

In addition to the $1.8 million granted by the Canada Council for the Arts in Newfoundland and Labrador in fiscal year 2006, nearly $100,000 in Public Lending Rights (PLR) payments was directed to

Bio FUNNY GIRL MARY WALSH

Mary Walsh is one of Newfoundland and Labrador's most recognized exports. She has been tickling Canadians' funny bones since the 1970s with her biting and clever humour.

The seventh of the eight children, Walsh had a difficult childhood growing up in 1950s St. John's. When she was just eight months old, she caught pneumonia and was sent to live with relatives. An arrangement that was supposed to be temporary became permanent, and she was raised by her aunt and uncle while the rest of her family lived next door. This separation gave Walsh a sense of being on the outside looking in. In her own words, she felt as though she had been "given away." It weighed heavily on her, and compounded the struggles that go with the teenage years. Her sense of humour helped her cope during difficult years and, as she says, her good and bad times are part and parcel of who she is.

Following a summer stint with CBC radio in St. John's, Walsh became a member of the Newfoundland Travelling Theatre Company (NTTC). She went off to study drama in Toronto, where the NTTC gang lured her into joining their production of "Cod on a Stick" at the Theatre Passe Muraille. A huge success, it eventually led to other

229 authors in the province.

- Number of members of the Writer's Alliance of Newfoundland and Labrador: 366
- Number of book publishers: 4 members of the Newfoundland and Labrador Publishers Association, and several minor and special interest publishers
- Approximate value of the book selling industry: $2 million
- Number of authors nominated for the Governor General's Literary Award: 10
- Number who have won: 2

ensemble productions, including the wildly popular "CODCO," which aired on CBC from 1988 to 1993. She participated in other ways as well—involving herself in the management of the LSPU Hall (now the Resource Centre for the Arts) in St. John's, writing the play "Hockey Wives" (1988), working with the Canadian Conference on the Arts, and collaborating on a number of CBC programs.

Mary Walsh was the original creative force behind TV's "This Hour Has 22 Minutes." In 1993 she successfully pitched the concept, assembled a good cast, and has been a mainstay of the program since the beginning. With her signature characters Marg Delahunty, Dakey Dunn and Miss Eulalia, she comments insightfully and hilariously on local politics and international affairs and everything in between.

This prolific actor, writer and producer has been in over 20 films, including "Random Passage," "New Waterford Girl," and "Mambo Italiano." She also turned heads and pages with her weekly, post-"22 Minutes" literary program "Mary Walsh: Open Book." In 2005, she launched "Hatching, Matching and Dispatching," a television comedy-drama, and made her feature-film directorial debut with "Young Triffie" in 2006.

Bio WRITING NEWFOUNDLAND VERSE: E.J. PRATT

E.J. (Edwin John) Pratt, one of Newfoundland's most acclaimed men of letters, was an ordained minister, a professor, a poet, and a literary critic. His life in and around the outports of Newfoundland and Labrador is reflected in his most celebrated works.

He was born in 1882, the son of a preacher in Western Bay in Conception Bay; his father's mission took the family along the coast to various communities. In 1904, after a brief teaching career, Pratt followed in his father's footsteps and became a candidate for the ministry. He was ordained in the Methodist Church in 1913 but never worked as a minister, opting instead to return to teaching. He landed a job in the English department at Victoria College (University of Toronto), where he stayed until 1953.

Poetry was one of Pratt's first and lasting loves. He began publishing his poems in 1914, but made his first significant waves in the arts community when he published *Newfoundland Verse* in 1923. This work earned him a reputation as one of the foremost poets in Canada and abroad. During his career his writing continued to win him honours, including the Royal Society of Canada's Lorne Pierce Medal for Poetry in 1940 and the Governor General's Award in 1937, 1940 and 1952. King George VI made him a Companion of the Order of St. Michael and St. George in 1946, in recognition of his contribution to arts in the Commonwealth.

Pratt served as editor of the prestigious *Canadian Poetry Magazine* from 1936 to 1943. Apart from *Newfoundland Verse*, his poetry rarely mentioned Newfoundland and Labrador explicitly; yet his work, steeped in references to the sea and maritime life, reflects his coastal upbringing. He belonged to no school or poetic movement, and relied on his own tastes, methods and styles, yet his work was highly regarded and influential during his lifetime. E.J. Pratt died in Toronto on April 26, 1964.

They Said It

"You can't come to a location like Newfoundland with preconceived ideas of where to put the camera or how to film a scene."
— **Swedish film director, Lasse Hallstrom, director of *The Shipping News*.**

THE SCOTIA BANK GILLER PRIZE

Several books by Newfoundland and Labrador have made the long and short lists for Canada's lucrative Scotiabank Giller Prize. Wayne Johnston has had three works so honoured: *Colony of Unrequited Dreams* in 1998, *The Navigator of New York* in 2002, and *The Custodian of Paradise* in 2006. In 2001, Michael Crummey's *River Thieves* was on the short list, and Lisa Moore made the top five in 2002 for *Open* and again in 2005 for *Alligator*. Kenneth J. Harvey's *Inside* was on the 2006 long list, as was Russell Wangersky's short story collection *The Hour of Bad Decisions*. Michael Winter's novel *The Architects Are Here* was on the 2007 long list. So far, however, no one has brought the prestigious prize home to the Rock.

Did you know...

that the A1C postal region in downtown St. John's boasts 250 artists, representing 3.3 percent of the area's total labour force? That rate comes in at four times higher than the national average and represents the second highest concentration of artists in the Atlantic Provinces.

> *"There is something very, very unique about Newfoundland — it has this enormously biblical quality about it, a very powerful and majestic quality."*
> — **Artist Anne Meredith Barry, 1932-2003.**

ARTS SPENDING

The people of Newfoundland and Labrador shelled out over $300 million for the arts in 2003-04, representing 3.3 percent of all the money spent that year. In comparison, all three levels of government offered up money for the arts to the tune of $96.1 million. This was the third-lowest arts spending in Canada — after Alberta ($170 million) and New Brunswick ($176 million) — amounting to $185 per person.

Source: Canada Council; Statistics Canada.

MUSIC INDUSTRY

- Annual value of the province's music industry: $40 million
- Number of members of the Music Industry Association of Newfoundland and Labrador: 700
- Number of symphonies: 2 (Newfoundland & Labrador Symphony Orchestra and the Newfoundland & Labrador Youth Orchestra)

Source: Music Industry Association of Newfoundland and Labrador.

Did you know...

that St. John's-born actress and model Shannon Tweed has appeared in more than 60 films since getting her big break as Playboy's Playmate of the Year in 1982? She and her partner Gene Simmons of rock band KISS have two children.

Take 5 TONY PLOUGHMAN'S TOP FIVE
MUSICAL ARTISTS

As many of its residents will tell you, downtown St. John's is blessed — it has one of the country's most interesting and celebrated independent music stores: Fred's Records. Tony Ploughman is the assistant manager and the principal purchaser for Fred's. His two dozen years with the store have given him a deep grasp of — and appreciation for — the range of exciting music in the province. Here are his top five performing and recording artists … and the reasons why.

1. **Duane Andrews:** The most celebrated artist to emerge from this province in the past five years is this guitarist extraordinaire. His music is vibrant, colourful, bedazzling — as the many regional and international accolades he has already received attest.

2. **Hey rosetta!:** The darlings on the local circuit are also receiving critical acclaim beyond it. Hey rosetta! creates textured, opulent alternative pop music—not unlike Arcade Fire or Coldplay.

3. **Amelia Curran:** This St. John's singer/songwriter has been the biggest selling independent female artist in the province the past two years (four CDs released, another on the way). Poetic, visceral, pensive, her music and evocative lyrics have been favourably compared to Leonard Cohen, Tracy Chapman, and Suzanne Vega.

4. **Shanneyganock:** They've been the life of the party for ten years or so now. A traditional band with a pulsating rhythm section, they're always popular on the bar circuit and are continuing to stretch out.

5. **Quintessential Vocal Ensemble:** Under the astute guidance of conductor Susan Quinn, this choir (a.k.a. QVE) has won international awards for its exquisitely arranged recordings. They are known and highly regarded in choral circles around the world.

Rounding out the list, two honorary mentions for stellar individual artists Blair Harvey and Mary Barry.

Take 5 KARL WELLS'S TOP FIVE
RESTAURANT PICKS

A career television, radio, and print journalist, Karl Wells is widely known for his 29-year tenure as CBC TV's "Here & Now" weather reporter. A self-acknowledged lifelong foodie, he has produced many food segments for local and national television programs. Currently, Karl is the restaurant critic for The Telegram, *the only province-wide daily newspaper in Newfoundland and Labrador. He is a restaurant panelist for* enRoute *magazine and a member of the North American Association of Food Journalists. He has been a judge at many amateur and professional cooking competitions— and is a student of the art of cooking himself.*

1. **The Vault Restaurant and Champagne Bar, 291 Water St., St. John's:** A superb restaurant with outstanding service and excellent French-influenced food.

2. **Atlantica, Portugal Cove:** Voted the top new restaurant in Canada for 2007 by *enRoute* magazine, Atlantica serves dishes influenced by traditional recipes and fresh ingredients.

3. **Basho, 283 Duckworth St., St John's:** A modern restaurant with an equally modern menu featuring perfectly prepared Japanese fusion cuisine.

4. **Bianca's, 171 Water St., St. John's:** A consistently good restaurant with excellent, freshly prepared Mediterranean cuisine and an exceptional wine list.

5. **The Cellar, 152 Water St., St. John's:** The city's longest established fine-dining restaurant, with smart service, a comfortable atmosphere and beautifully prepared meals. Fresh seafood is often featured.

Did you know...

that Canada's first Subway restaurant opened in June 1986 in St. John's?

DINING
- Number of restaurants, bars and caterers in the province: 996
- Number of people employed in the industry: 13,200
- Industry sales in 2006: $411 million
- Industry's share of provincial GDP: 2.3 percent

Sources: Canadian Restaurant and Foodservices Association; Hospitality Newfoundland and Labrador.

FAST FOOD
- Number of McDonald's in Canada 1,400
- In Newfoundland and Labrador: 27
- Number of Tim Horton's in Canada: 2,823
- In Newfoundland and Labrador: 56
- Number of Subways in Canada: 2,321
- In Newfoundland and Labrador: 32

SPIRITS
- Number of wineries: 3
- Approximate number of bottles of wine produced annually: 400,000
- Number of micro-breweries: 4
- Bottles of beer produced annually: 1.3 million bottles

Source: Government of Newfoundland and Labrador.

They Said It

"When I think of St. John's, it's like the capital of the world for fish and chips."

— Memorial University professor and author Maura Hanrahan.

The Royal St. John's Regatta

The isolated, cash-strapped, and church-centred Newfoundland society of days gone by was the backdrop for annual summer fundraising parties, usually under Church auspices, that promised a day of fun, games, food, music, and, above all, a chance to socialize. Originally held on a Sunday when most people were free from work — after dutifully attending church services, of course — such events, called "Garden Parties," grew into annual regattas in many communities.

The oldest of these festive events — indeed one of the oldest sporting events in North America — is the annual Royal St. John's Regatta, first held in 1818. Weather permitting, it is still held on the first Wednesday in August. Each year as many as 50,000 spectators gather on the shores of Quidi Vidi Lake, located in the east end of the city, to enjoy the amateur races and the socializing that accompanies them.

Dubbed "The Largest Garden Party in the World," the Regatta once offered visitors a chance to spin the "Wheel of Chocolate," to challenge a "Greasy Pole" or catch a "Greasy Pig." The Regatta has missed few beats in its near two-centuries-old history. There were no races during most of the 1860s thanks to political and religious friction in the colony; in 1892 it was cancelled because the lakeshore area was being used for temporary housing for people displaced by the city's Great Fire; and the 1914 merriment was dampened by the outbreak of war across the Atlantic.

During the years 1915 to 1918, out of respect for those fighting in the war, no Regattas were held. The practice of "no Regatta during war" was again observed in 1940, but the event was resumed the following year, as it felt it would entertain and help keep fit the troops stationed nearby.

Today the Regatta remains an important social holiday — and is the only civic holiday in the country that is declared by a non-governmental committee and is solely dependent on the weather.

Did you know...

that the first baseball games in St. John's (1929) were played indoors at Prince's Rink?

THE GEORGE STREET FESTIVAL

Perhaps the one thing that puts and keeps St. John's in the minds of those who like a little revelry when they travel is the city's famed George Street, which is believed to offer more pubs and bars per square foot than any other street in North America. George Street is a mecca for those looking for everything from traditional Newfoundland fiddle-fests to the latest local rock bands.

Entertainment lights up George Street year round, but the best time to celebrate is during the George Street Festival. For six days and nights in August, access to George Street is restricted, and some of the province's finest musical acts perform on the specially constructed street stage.

Everyone who is anyone has performed at the festival, including local favourites such as Great Big Sea, the Irish Descendants and Sam Roberts. An entrance fee provides access to the entire festival, including the pubs. Drinking is permitted on the street so many spend their days and nights weaving in and out of bars. This is one festival not to be missed.

Did you know...

that two women's teams competed in the 1856 Royal St. John's Regatta, but women did not compete again until the 1940s?

Did you know...

that Mary Ewing Outerbridge introduced lawn tennis to North America in 1874? The Newfoundlander introduced it to her brother in Staten Island, after she had seen it played in Bermuda.

Screeching In

Newfoundlanders and Labradorians have a reputation for being friendly and adept at making people "from away" feel at home. Visitors can even be made "honorary Newfoundlanders" in a ritual called "Screeching in." Initially a rum home-made by adding water to the residue in empty molasses barrels, today's Screech is a potent dark rum produced by the Newfoundland Liquor Commission. Legend has it that one American's taste buds were so offended by the caustic swill that he let out a howl; when someone asked what the terrible screech was, the bartender said: " 'Tis the rum, me son."

For nearly three decades, the "Screech-in" has been a popular and highly marketed tradition. Initiation begins with the visitor being sponsored by a born-and-bred Newfoundlander who immediately asks the initiate to kiss a cod (or in some places, to pucker up to a puffin's arse). With a holler of "long may your big jib draw" ('long may you have fair winds/good fortune') and the downing of a burning shot of Screech, one becomes an honorary Newfoundlander with a certificate to prove it.

While this tradition is well known and mostly appreciated as good clean fun, it is not without controversy. Some think it supports a stereotype that reduces Newfoundlanders and Labradorians to people concerned with little more than alcohol and a good time. Former Premier Clyde Wells even went so far as to remove his name from "Screech-in" certificates during his tenure in office.

Opponents tried to find other ceremonies to affectionately inflict on visitors but nothing could take the place of the "Screech-in," an exercise that remains a comical rite of passage for many tourists.

Did you know...

that the band Newfoundland-born 2005 Canadian Idol runner-up Rex Goudie formed in high school was called "Purple Monkey Bomb Squad"?

SPORTS

Newfoundland and Labrador takes sports seriously. Like the rest of Canada, one of its strongest passions is for hockey (even though St. John's lost its Quebec Major Junior Hockey League team — the Fog Devils — after the 2007-08 season), but it also has unusually strong and long (for Canada) high school and amateur soccer, rugby, and basketball traditions.

Newfoundland and Labrador's sports accomplishments recently reached the highest rung. The province's shining moment on the world stage came in the 2006 Winter Olympics in Torino, Italy, when the St. John's-based Brad Gushue rink took the gold medal in men's curling.

Also on the amateur level, in recent years Memorial University's women's basketball team has more than once won the Atlantic Provinces title and contended for national honours. And though the St. John's Regatta may not attract worldwide notice, for the midsummer weeks leading up to the annual August rowing races, the events unfolding on Quidi Vidi Lake are never far from the attention of the province's sports fans.

Did you know...

that it took the makers of "Faustus Bidgood" so long to make this shoestring-budget but much-treasured film that the child that appears in some scenes is the same one that a pregnant woman is expecting in others?

The province has an active provincial sports body, a provincial sports hall of fame, and the construction of a $6.3 million provincial training facility is under way in St. John's. The new facility will provide space for the province's athletes to improve their skills and prepare for competition, and also increase the ability of local sports organizations to attract provincial, regional, national, and even international events.

Take 5 FIVE CULTURAL EVENTS
NOT TO MISS

1. St. John's International Women's Film Festival
2. The Sound Symposium
3. Festival 500
4. St. John's Folk Festival
5. The March Hare

Weblinks

Rick Mercer's Blog

www.rickmercer.blogspot.com/

An absolutely hilarious blog written by a political satirist extraordinaire, Newfoundland and Labrador's own Rick Mercer.

Newfoundland Independent Film Cooperative

www.nifco.org/about.asp.html

Find out what's going on in the vibrant world of Newfoundland film and filmmaking.

Best of Newfoundland Music

www.wordplay.com/music/

Read up on the province's recording artists or download some music of Newfoundland and Labrador at this interactive website.

The Rooms Provincial Art Gallery, Archives, and Museum

www.therooms.ca/

Find out about exhibitions, lectures, activities, and other events taking place at the province's impressive cultural hub in St. John's.

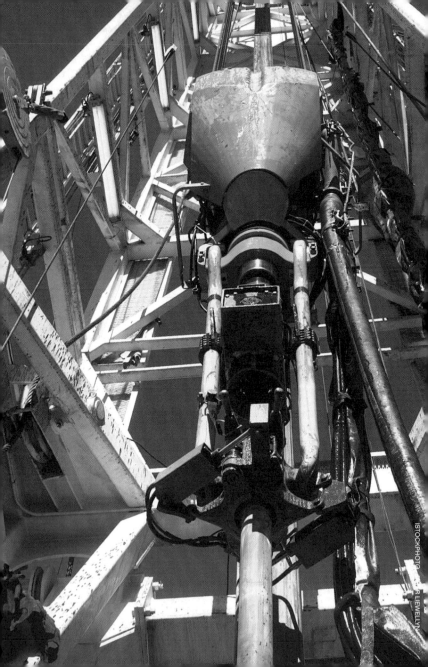

Economy

Newfoundland and Labrador's original and seemingly endless resource was codfish. It ruled commerce for 300 years until the late 1800s, when land-based resource enterprises were added to the mix. Today's substantial pulp and paper, timber harvesting, and mining industries have their roots in this phase of development.

After joining Confederation, the economy of Canada's "newest province" featured low incomes, high unemployment, and fears of declining cod stocks. A moratorium on fishing for Atlantic cod was imposed in 1992 and has not been lifted. This staggering blow has ongoing implications, but the fishery sector recovered by turning to aquaculture and to other species — particularly crab and shrimp. In 2007, the total landed value in the fisheries sector was $478.7 million.

Other resources are today's prime economic generators, however. Several important mega-projects are now online — notably in offshore oil and nickel extraction (Voisey's Bay); in 2007 the mining sector's exploration expenditure reached a record $138 million. The province negotiated an equity stake in offshore oil development (134 million barrels produced in '07); with high oil prices this was expected to further increase the industry's giant contribution to the province's coffers.

In addition, high-tech industries (chiefly in St. John's) and tourism now add significant income and activity. Looking to the future, the province is investing in a long-term Energy Plan that will include development of the lower Churchill River in Labrador.

GROSS DOMESTIC PRODUCT

A province's Gross Domestic Product (GDP) measures the total value of goods and services it produces. In 2006, Newfoundland and Labrador's GDP was $25.6 billion.

- Per capita GDP: $50,244
- GDP growth from 1999 to 2006: 110 percent
- Canadian GDP per capita: $44,333
- Canadian GDP growth from 1999 to 2006: 47 percent

TAXES

- Provincial sales tax: 8 percent
- GST (federal sales tax): 5 percent
- Personal income tax rate: 8.7 percent on first $39,215
  - 13.8 percent on next $30,214
  - 16.5 percent on amounts over $63,429
- Small business tax rate: 5 percent
- Corporate tax rate: 14 percent

Source: Canada Customs and Revenue Agency, NL Dept. of Finance, Canada Revenue Agency.

TAX FREEDOM DAY

Tax freedom day (date on which earnings no longer go to taxes, 2008) is June 19 nationally.

- Alberta: June 1
- New Brunswick: June 14
- Prince Edward Island: June 14

Did you know...

that 1993 holds the unhappy record for the highest unemployment level in the province's history, when it peaked at 20.4 percent?

- Saskatchewan: June 14
- Manitoba: June 16
- British Columbia: June 16
- Ontario: June 19
- Nova Scotia: June 19
- Newfoundland and Labrador: July 1
- Quebec: July 26

PERSONAL INCOME
- Newfoundland and Labrador's per capita income (2006): $30,935
- St. John's per capita income (2007): $29,100
- St. John's average household income (2007): $72,600
- Canada's per capita income (2007): $38,200

Sources: NL Statistics, City of St. John's.

BY THE HOUR
In January 2008, workers in Newfoundland earned an average hourly salary of $18.77, up 9.3 percent from January 2007.
- Aged 15 to 24: $10.58
- Aged 25 to 54: $20.06
- Aged 55 and older: $19.71
- Men: $20.55
- Women: $17.11
- Part-time: $13.75
- Full-time: $19.78
- Unionized: $22.52
- Non-unionized: $15.93

Source: Statistics Canada.

SMALL BUSINESS (LESS THAN 50 EMPLOYEES)
Small businesses as a percentage of total businesses: 93.7
Small business employment as a percentage of total employment: 36
Number of small businesses with 1-4 employees: (percent) 76.9

5-19 employees: (percent) 13.2
20-49 employees: (percent) 3.6
50-499 employees: (percent) 3.8
500 + employees: (percent) 2.5

The Crosbie Dynasty

For more than 150 years, the Crosbie name has been synonymous with the economic fortunes of Newfoundland and Labrador. In 1858, a young George Graham Crosbie left his family in New Brunswick to try his luck in Newfoundland. In 1862, he married Martha Ellen Chalker and the couple and their eight children made their home in Brigus. It was here the Crosbie empire began with George's store and sawmill.

When the 1880s brought hard times, the Crosbies moved to St. John's where George purchased and renovated the posh Central Hotel. In 1892, the hotel went up in smoke in the Great Fire. Undaunted, George rebuilt an even grander hotel. In 1895, just three months after the new hotel opened, George died at age 59.

John Chalker Crosbie, George's youngest son, was only 19 at the time, but he stepped into his father's shoes, honouring him by renaming the new hotel the Crosbie Hotel. He turned to the fish export business in 1900, and Crosbie and Company soon became a major exporter of fish in Newfoundland. (The hotel was sold in 1933 after a turn under sister Ellie's watch.)

When John turned to politics, he used his business acumen as Shipping and then Finance Minister to raise the sagging fortunes of the Newfoundland economy (and, some say, to add to his own coffers). In 1925, a year after retiring from politics, he started the

SELF-EMPLOYMENT

As of January 2008, 27,700 Newfoundlanders and Labradorians were self-employed.

Source: Statistics Canada

Newfoundland Butter Company, which he ran until his death in 1932. His son Chesley carried on the family business, adding herring processing.

When the herring industry faltered in the 1950s, Chesley diversified and established a shipping company, bought into a construction effort and also into Eastern Provincial Airlines. Everything he touched succeeded. When he died in 1962, his brother Percy and son Andrew — the man who would later become the 'czar' of the Crosbie empire (and the brother of the province's current Lieutenant Governor, John Crosbie) — expanded the family's enterprises exponentially. By 1976, the Crosbie family controlled 24 businesses in the province and eight in Ontario and Quebec; all told the family was worth $100 million.

In the 1970s, the family (literally) struck oil and established Crosbie Offshore Services and associated companies. However, finding oil did not protect the Crosbie fortunes from mismanagement. In 1989, criminal charges of fraud were laid against Andrew. In 1991, before his case was heard in court, he lost his battle with cancer. Today, Andrew's children — Alex, Robert, Timothy and Cynthia — maintain the family's business interests in more trying economic times than those of their predecessors.

Take 5 DR. WADE LOCKE'S TOP FIVE
ECONOMIC TRENDS

An economist by training, with a Ph.D. from McMaster University, Wade Locke is a professor at Memorial University of Newfoundland. He is also the past president of the Atlantic Canada Economics Association and a senior policy advisor to the Atlantic Provinces Economic Council. Dr. Locke has an extensive research record in a variety of areas, but primarily focuses on natural resources and public finances (broadly defined). His research and teaching record is bolstered by his knowledge and understanding of the Newfoundland and Labrador economy.

1. **The diversification of Newfoundland and Labrador's economic activity into offshore oil production:** Since the first barrel of oil was produced here in 1997, the value of economic activity in Newfoundland and Labrador has increased to an estimated $24.9 billion in 2006, up 237 percent from $10.5 billion in 1996. The additional funds flowing into the treasury have enabled the provincial government to record its first real surplus since entering Confederation, while simultaneously addressing social and economic problems that have plagued the province for years, and not compromising the long-term financial viability of the province.

2. **The collapse of the cod fishery in the early 1990s and subsequent moratorium:** Not only did this remove the economic livelihood of thousands of Newfoundlanders and Labradorians, it had its most devastating effects in rural parts of the province where alternate economic opportunities were scarce. Dealing with the crisis has proved difficult and has led large numbers of people to leave Newfoundland and Labrador to seek employment opportunities elsewhere.

3. **Outmigration:** From 1981 to 1992, outmigration averaged about 2,600 people per year, but after 1992 that number reached 5,000 annually. Consequently, the province's population declined by 63,000, from a high of 580,000 in 1993 to 517,000 in 2004. This has had implications for financial support received from the federal government and has required an adjustment of the social priorities of the provincial government, as aspects of the infrastructure, such as the school system, are no longer able to effectively match the needs of the province. This, in turn, has required restructuring — such as school closures — and added the social tension and disruption that accompanies it.

4. **Aging population and young workers outmigrating:** It is projected that Newfoundland and Labrador's labour market will experience a serious skilled-labour shortage in the next five to 10 years. An aging population does not have the ability to replicate itself, and the implication for future population growth is negative. As well, if new entrants to the work force leave, then the absence of a critical resource — skilled labour — will act as an impediment to the future development of Newfoundland and Labrador. This, in turn, will reinforce the outmigration that results from a need to look for employment opportunities, and will compound the aging labour-force problem.

5. **The rural/urban divide:** There is a growing disparity in economic opportunities and outlook between rural and urban parts of the province. The population in St. John's is younger than in the province as a whole, earns higher average incomes, and has lower levels of unemployment. One implication is that people are moving from the rural parts of the province to the more urban parts, which, in turn, further exacerbates rural/urban disparities. While urbanization is a worldwide phenomenon, it is more pronounced in Newfoundland and Labrador than in other parts of Canada.

UNEMPLOYMENT
As of January 2008, unemployment stood at 14.6 percent, the highest in Canada. Nationally, the unemployment rate is 6.3 percent.
- Lowest unemployment rate in Newfoundland and Labrador: St. John's, 6.8 percent
- Highest unemployment rate in Newfoundland and Labrador: Burin Peninsula and South Coast, 17.6 percent

Source: NL Statistics Agency.

BUYING A HOUSE
As of December 2007, the average house price in Newfoundland was $163,276, up from $141,632 a year before. Regionally, prices vary. Houses in St. John's average $149,258 while homes in Happy Valley-Goose Bay average $120,000. Nationally, the average price of buying a home was $317,825 in December 2007 — an increase of slightly more than 14 percent over the December 2006, average of $278,573.

AVERAGE HOUSE PRICES NATIONALLY

Newfoundland and Labrador	$163,276
New Brunswick	$164,160
Saskatchewan	$299,285
Manitoba	$169,377
Prince Edward Island	$137,170
Nova Scotia	$172,014
Quebec	$220,089
Alberta	$354,290
Ontario	$317,346
British Columbia	$457,865

Source: Canadian Real Estate Association.

Did you know...

that Newfoundland and Labrador led the country in economic growth in 2006?

You Said How Much?

All figures are hourly and are drawn from the latest available data — experienced and non-experienced workers.

Dentists	$102.56	$51.28
Electrical and electronics engineers	$40.29	$21.16
Pharmacists	$40.00	$25.00
Mechanical engineers	$37.86	$19.80
Lawyers	$37.34	$20.85
Commissioned police officers	$36.99	$34.70
Civil engineers	$36.00	$21.00
Secondary school teachers	$35.98	$20.97
Social workers	$35.69	$23.89
Probation and parole officers	$35.17	$24.20
Elementary school teachers	$34.93	$20.36
Information systems analysts & consultants	$34.52	$22.26
Registered nurses	$34.48	$23.48
Crane operators	$34.08	$22.27
Conservation and fishery officers	$30.65	$17.75
Fire fighters	$32.63	$14.83
Occupational therapists	$30.50	$25.50
Geologists, geochemists and geophysicists	$30.00	$21.00
Electricians	$26.80	$18.00
Deck crew (ship transport)	$23.73	$19.76
Physiotherapists	$23.00	$20.00
Truck drivers	$22.36	$13.50
Letter carriers	$22.18	$20.73
Graphic designers	$20.50	$12.55
Financial auditors and accountants	$20.36	$17.81
Bricklayers	$20.00	$14.00
Sheet metal workers	$19.15	$14.00
Secretaries	$18.65	$12.50
Plumbers	$15.37	$9.00
Journalist	$15.00	$11.00
General office clerk	$15.00	$9.00
Painters and decorators	$15.00	$8.00
Construction trades helpers & labourers	$10.10	$8.75
Early childhood educators and assistants	$10.00	$7.50
Retail salespersons	$9.30	$7.50
Service station attendants	$8.75	$8.00

Source: Human Resources and Development Canada.

(AVERAGE WEEKLY PAY CHEQUE)

1. **Finance and insurance** ($975.53)
2. **Professional, scientific, and technical services** ($929.97)
3. **Information and cultural industries** ($885.83)
4. **Goods-producing industries** ($883.28)
5. **Manufacturing** ($818.19)

Source: Government of Newfoundland and Labrador.

RENTING

- Percentage of Newfoundlanders who rent: 21.1 percent
- Average monthly rent paid: $550
- Average monthly rent in St. John's: $650
- Average vacancy rate: 4.1 percent

HOW WE GET TO WORK

- 86.3 percent drive
- 1.9 percent use public transit
- 7.7 percent walk
- 0.3 percent bicycle

Source: Statistics Canada.

GOVERNMENT DOUGH (2007)

- Total provincial revenue: $5.3 billion
- Percentage of Canada's total revenue provided by Newfoundland: 1.7
- Value of federal transfer payments to Newfoundland: $2.2 billion
- Percentage of provincial coffers that comes from various federal sources: 40
- Amount of revenue coming from provincial sources: $3.1 billion
- Percentage of provincial revenues coming from provincial sources: 60

Sources: Government of Newfoundland and Labrador; Statistics Canada.

Take 5 TOP FIVE SECTORS

IN WHICH NEWFOUNDLANDERS AND LABRADORIANS WORK

1. **Sales and service**
2. **Business, finance, and administrative**
3. **Trades, transport, equipment operation**
4. **Social sciences, education, government services, religion**
5. **Health**

Source: Statistics Canada.

WHERE THE PROVINCE GETS ITS MONEY (2008 ESTIMATES)

- Personal income tax: 20.0 percent
- Sales tax: 17.4 percent
- Offshore royalties: 25.4 percent
- Corporate income tax: 8.5 percent
- Gasoline tax: 3.7 percent
- Tobacco tax: 2.8 percent
- Lottery revenues: 2.4 percent
- Newfoundland Liquor Corporation: 2.8 percent
- Payroll tax: 2.6 percent
- Other: 16.8 percent

Source: Government of Newfoundland and Labrador.

Did you know...

that in 2001, estimates showed that one third of Alberta's Fort MacMurray population hailed from Newfoundland and Labrador?

Did you know...

that economists estimate that Newfoundland and Labrador will soon produce almost half of Canada's conventional light crude oil?

WHERE THE MONEY GOES

Newfoundland and Labrador households spent an average of $53,939 in 2006. Here's how it broke down:

- Income tax: $10,074 (18.7 percent)
- Shelter: $8,605 (16 percent)
- Transportation: $7,824 (14.5 percent)
- Food: $6,322 (11.7 percent)
- Insurance/pension payments: $3,202 (5.9 percent)
- Household operation: $2,973 (5.5 percent)
- Clothing: $2,622 (4.9 percent)
- Monetary gifts/contributions: $1,143 (2.1 percent)
- Health care: $1,510 (2.8 percent)
- Tobacco and alcohol: $1,628 (3 percent)
- Education: $705 (1.3 percent)
- Personal care: $1,021 (1.9 percent)
- Reading material: $199 (0.4 percent)
- Games of chance: $280 (0.5 percent)

Source: Statistics Canada.

GOVERNMENT DEBT (2007)

- Total debt: $11.5 billion
- The per capita debt load of Newfoundland: $22,700

GOVERNMENT EMPLOYMENT (2007)

- Total number of people who work for government: 54,321
- Federal general government: 7,161
- Provincial government: 11,301
- Health /social service institutions: 16,552
- Universities, colleges, vocational and trade institutions: 6,575
- Local general government: 4,091
- Local school boards: 8,641

Source: Government of Newfoundland and Labrador.

OFFSHORE OIL AND GAS

Newfoundland and Labrador's offshore oil industry has helped offset the economic devastation wrought by the 1992 cod moratorium. By 2004, it earned $6 billion annually. Almost 16 percent of provincial revenue comes from offshore royalties, and this is poised to increase. In 2007, the province's offshore oil wells produced about 135 million barrels with a value of more than $10.3 billion, an increase of 26.6 percent over 2006.

Source: NL Department of Finance.

DIGGING DEEP

- Year in which the first oil well was drilled offshore: 1966
- Number of sites "spudded" (initial drilling) to date: 318
- Number of oil wells discovered to date: 16
- Number of gas wells discovered: 7

Did you know...

that Newfoundlanders and Labradorians are very generous? In 2006, the average donor's total income ($35,400) was the lowest in Canada, and yet their charitable donations were $330, the third highest in the nation.

> "Newfoundland needs to make its economic pie bigger. As we all know, our pie is too small and too many people are fighting for a piece of it. Indeed, too many Newfoundlanders and Labradorians are going elsewhere to get their just desserts. We have to find a way to reverse our fortunes and to do so at home."
> — **Vic Young, former head of FPI and Labrador Hydro and former Deputy Minister of Finance, at a natural resources exhibition in 2002.**

WELL, WELL, WELL

Newfoundland has three main oil well projects (number of barrels produced in 2007.)

- Hibernia (49.2 million)
- Terra Nova (42.4 million)
- White Rose (42.8 million)

MINING

- In 2007, the value of the mining industry: $2.5 billion
- Percentage of Newfoundland and Labrador's GDP that comes from mining: 3.2
- Number of Newfoundlanders and Labradorians who work in the mining industry: 3,290
- Percentage of total labour force working in this industry: 1.6
- Most-mined mineral: Iron ore (at 20 million tonnes, just over 50% of all ore mined)

Source: Government of Newfoundland and Labrador.

Did you know...

that Newfoundlander and Labradorian hourly wage earners work 30.5 hours per week, the second-lowest of any Canadian province?

Take 5 TOP FIVE
INDUSTRY EXPORTS

1. **Heavy petroleum oil**
2. **Light petroleum oil**
3. **Iron ore**
4. **Newsprint**
5. **Frozen crab**

Source: www.nlbusiness.ca.

MANUFACTURING

- Percentage of the province's GDP that manufacturing accounts for: 5 percent
- Annual amount generated by export of manufactured goods: $4.3 billion
- Top three manufacturing industries in Newfoundland and Labrador: food processing, newsprint manufacturing, and petroleum refining
- Percentage of total labour force working in this industry: 7

Sources: Government of Newfoundland and Labrador.

FISHING

Since the 1992 cod moratorium, Newfoundland and Labrador's fishing industry has been transformed. Despite a much reduced cod catch, a restructured fishery featuring other species (primarily crab and shrimp) contributes much to provincial coffers. In 2007, the province's seafood industry contributed over $1 billion in production value.

- Number of commercial aquaculture site licences: 99
- Number of fish processing plants: 143
- Number of jobs the fishing industry creates in peak season: 24,805
- Number of boats these fishers use: 8,709
- Number of boats that fish the inshore: 7,640 under 35'
- Number of licences for the various types of fisheries: 32,577

Sources: Fisheries and Oceans Canada, NL Department of Fisheries.

SHELLFISH INDUSTRY

Since the moratorium, shellfish has become the most important species in the Newfoundland and Labrador fishery. Shrimp and crab are the two top fish exports.

- Shellfish haul in 2007: 189,158 tonnes
- Value of shellfish in 2007: $382.9 million
- Shrimp haul in 2007: 115,605 tonnes

Cohen's Home Furnishing Ltd.

The Cohen family and their furniture stores are main characters in one of Newfoundland and Labrador's most successful business stories. At the turn of the 20th century, Simon Cohen, his wife, and three young sons left England for St. John's, where Simon took up work with the Newfoundland Clothing Company.

After a 15-year hiatus in the United States, Cohen and his brood, now numbering seven, returned to Newfoundland. In 1919, Simon and his eldest son, Charles, opened a general store in Grand Falls Station (which is now known as Grand Falls-Windsor). By 1935, four other sons had joined the business, with Michael — son number three — acting as general manager. Just before Christmas 1945, a new Cohen's store under construction burned to the ground; the following August, Michael died of a heart attack.

Jack replaced his brother at the helm of the family enterprise; Michael's son Boyd soon stepped up to the plate as well. Boyd introduced furniture to the store's stock and turned the enterprise into a home-furnishings giant. Furniture sales took off, becoming the lynchpin of the business as the Cohen family embraced the concept of buying in bulk before it was in vogue.

By the time Boyd sold the business in 1985, it consisted of 13 stores. In 2005, in recognition of his successes and contributions, Boyd Cohen was inducted into the Newfoundland and Labrador Business Hall of Fame.

Take 5 TOP EXPORT MARKETS
IN 2006

1. **United States** (21 percent)
2. **China** (8 percent)
3. **Germany** (8 percent)
4. **Netherlands** (4 percent)
5. **United Kingdom** (4 percent)

Source: www.nlbusiness.ca.

- Total value: $155.1 million
- Snow crab haul in 2007: 50,165 tonnes
- Total value: $171.2 million

Sources: Government of Newfoundland and Labrador; Fisheries and Oceans Canada.

THE SEAL FISHERY

The province's seal fishery markets seal pelts, meat and oil. In 2006, it had a market value of $30.5 million, which dropped to $11.4 million in 2007 due to a massive decrease in the value of the pelts (from $102 to $55 per pelt). The 2007 NL quota for the Northwest Atlantic harp seal herd, estimated to number 5.5 million, was 270,000, while 2008's quota is set at 275,000.

Source: Government of Newfoundland and Labrador.

Take 5 TOP FIVE SHELLFISH/CRUSTACEAN
EXPORTS

1. **Queen crab**
2. **Shrimp**
3. **Soft shell clams**
4. **Lobster**
5. **Scallops**

Source: Fisheries and Oceans Canada.

Take 5 — TOP FIVE LANDED GROUNDFISH SPECIES (2007)

1. **Cod**
2. **Turbot**
3. **Flounder**
4. **Redfish**
5. **Hake**

Source: Government of Newfoundland and Labrador.

FORESTRY AND LOGGING

Nine million of the island's 15 million acres of forest are productive. The most productive zone covers 56 percent of the woodland in the western and central regions. Labrador has 13 million acres of productive forest, most of which is in the valleys of the Churchill, Alexis, Eagle and Kaipokok rivers.

- Most common softwood species: balsam fir and black spruce
- Most common hardwood species: white birch
- Approximate value of annual newspaper shipments: about $595 million
- Value of lumber production (2007): $43 million

Source: Heritage Newfoundland; Government of Newfoundland and Labrador.

TOURISM

- In 2006, tourism injected $366 million into the provincial economy.
- 496,400 people "from away" visited in 2006, up 5.6 percent over 2005.
- 349,700 non-resident visitors arrived by air, up 11% over 2005.
- The number of licenced B&Bs increased by almost 80% in the previous decade.
- The number of rooms available more than doubled in the same period.
- The top three regions of origin for people travelling to the province by car were the Maritimes, Ontario, and the U.S.

Source: Government of Newfoundland and Labrador.

Weblinks

Business Portal Website

http://www.business.gov.nl.ca/

A self-described "gateway to online information for business start-up, operation, relocating to the province, investment and exporting," this provincial government website is a valuable resource for the business-minded.

Innovation Strategy

http://www.intrd.gov.nl.ca/intrd/Innovation/default.htm

Also a provincial undertaking, this website is for businessmen and women who "think outside the box."

St. John's Economic Development

http://www.stjohns.ca/business/index.jsp

St. John's is the economic hub of the province. This city-managed website gives you the skinny on the city's economy, and offers insight to its economic potential. Links to important business agencies and organizations are very useful.

Politics

GOVERNMENT BEFORE GOVERNMENT

Newfoundland and Labrador's political and legal history got off to a rocky start. Viewing settlement as an impediment to the all-important fishery, Britain was not concerned with the colony's law and governance. Instead, for decades, the colony was "governed" by the Fishing Admiral system. The captain of the first ship to drop anchor in any harbour each spring earned the right to be Fishing Admiral and become the governor for the season.

Regardless of his legal training or education, the makeshift governor was empowered to act as judge and jury. He decided all legal matters, though not with impartiality. Decisions frequently supported his interests, and major offences often went unpunished.

Officials recognized that the system was not working. Although only a slight improvement, King William's Act of 1699 dictated that the commodore of the annual naval fleet would act as governor each year throughout his tenure. There was no longer a new leader each spring, but the fishery, not law and order, remained the top priority. As inadequate and ineffectual as it was, this form of governance remained in effect through the 18th century, as settlements began to be established and grow.

CALL FOR RESPONSIBLE GOVERNMENT

In the early 19th century, Newfoundlanders, egged on by enlightened European immigrants, called for the right to elect their own lawmakers in a system of representative government. The colony got its wish in 1832, although executive powers remained with the Crown.

Before long, Newfoundlanders were dissatisfied with the limited form of this representative government. Newfoundland's governing elite — merchants and entrepreneurs who seemed to care more for their own industry than the future of the colony — were accused of retarding the colony's political evolution. Religious strife was thrown into the mix, with appointed officials almost always belonging to the Church of England, while many of the elected representatives were Roman Catholic.

Elected officials — and those who put them there — wanted more: the independence that came with colonial status. In 1855, after several tense and violence-riddled decades, Britain granted Newfoundland responsible government. The colony's executive became "responsible" — they were chosen from elected members of the House of Assembly, and were answerable to the public's electoral endorsement.

DOMINION DAY

Newfoundland became an independent, self-governing dominion on September 26, 1907, the same day the colony of New Zealand won its independence.

CANADA CALLING

When New Brunswick, Nova Scotia, and the colonies of Upper and Lower Canada were discussing union, Newfoundland was also invited to join. But when the four first provinces struck their deal in 1867, Newfoundland wanted no part of it. The possibility of confederation, however, never completely left the agenda.

Between 1864 and 1949 the debate resurfaced several times, especially as the colony-cum-Dominion faced financial hardship. In 1869, anti-confederates won the first Confederation election, convincing

They Said It

"I never thought I'd see the day."
— Joseph R. (Joey) Smallwood in 1949
when Newfoundland became part of Canada.

Newfoundlanders they could prosper without the support of Canada.

Events of the 1930s conspired to make Confederation a more attractive prospect. That decade's Great Depression ravaged the Island's economy much as it did elsewhere in North America. In 1934, Newfoundland's system of responsible government collapsed along with the economy. In return for Britain's financial support, Newfoundland surrendered her governance to a British-appointed commission of seven (Commission of Government).

For 15 years, no elections were held and no legislature convened. It was into this political abyss that the issue of Confederation reemerged in the late 1940s. Although coy about its intentions, Canada was interested in Newfoundland and had the support of both Britain and a fiery and persuasive Newfoundlander named Joseph R. Smallwood. In 1948, Newfoundlanders had to choose their political future from three options:

• Return to responsible government as it existed in the years leading up to 1934
• Confederation with Canada
• Continuation of the Commission of Government

After a series of referendums, Newfoundlanders narrowly voted to join Confederation. On March 31, 1949, Newfoundlanders became Canadian citizens.

They Said It

"Newfoundland today enters Confederation as a full and equal partner with the older provinces. It is my hope and belief that in the future the advantages of the union will be increasingly recognized by the great majority of the people of Newfoundland and of all Canada."
— Louis St. Laurent, Prime Minister of Canada, 1949.

The Greatest Newfoundlander?

Newfoundland and Labrador's most loved and loathed politician, Joseph R. Smallwood, entered the world on Christmas Eve, 1900, in the small community of Gambo.

Smallwood got an early taste of public life as a newspaper apprentice. Interested in publishing and a life off the Island, a bespectacled 20-year-old Joey left for New York. During his five years in the city he met his wife Clara and worked for a socialist newspaper. This work gave him a powerful affinity for unions and workers' rights, and when he came home in 1925, he became a vociferous union organizer and publisher.

In 1928, Smallwood entered politics as campaign manager for Liberal Richard Squires. Squires's win earned Smallwood an appointment as a justice of the peace. Fully steeped in Liberal politics, Smallwood started the Liberal newspaper *The Watchdog.* Through the 1930s he was undeterred by his own electoral losses and continued to advise Liberals in the legislature.

For a decade he bided his time and embraced extra-political interests — he continued to organize labour, became a broadcaster with his own radio show ("From the Masthead") and established a pig farm. By 1946, Smallwood was a well-known figure in Newfoundland. He used his notoriety, and his access to the airwaves, to promote a cause near and dear to his heart: Confederation.

Joey Smallwood's belief that Confederation would bring prosperity to Newfoundland struck an appealing chord with many cash-strapped Newfoundlanders. In the 1948 provincial referendum a small majority voted to join Canada, and Smallwood became the first Liberal Premier of Canada's tenth province. For almost a quarter of a century, he ran the government of Newfoundland, some say with autocratic control over its economy and media.

Smallwood's critics charge that over time he became more interested in his own legacy than with the well-being of Newfoundland. Many have condemned his decision to relocate outport communities, while others have criticized him for abandoning workers' rights in favour of big business. He brushed off such criticisms and staunchly maintained that the economic and social development of Newfoundland was always his top priority.

As proof he offered a host of projects completed during his tenure: roads and an electric grid were established, Memorial University became a degree-granting institution, and his brainchild – *The Encyclopedia of Newfoundland and Labrador* – chronicled the province's history in unprecedented depth.

Despite the fact that he had resigned from Smallwood's cabinet because of his leader's authoritarianism, former premier Clyde Wells once asserted that Smallwood was "perhaps the greatest Newfoundlander that ever lived." While many Newfoundlanders and Labradorians would agree, probably an equal number would not. Regardless, it is undeniable that "the little man from Gambo" forever changed Newfoundland and Labrador.

"Fifty seven years ago on March 31 just before the stroke of midnight, my family's country was signed away. Newfoundland and Labrador joined Canada. It was a mistake."
— **Liam O'Brien of Buchans, Newfoundland and Labrador.**

CONSPIRACY THEORY OF CONFEDERATION

The vote in favour of Confederation was narrow — when the final numbers were tallied, just 52 percent had said "yes." Many of the remaining 48 percent refused to accept the results. Anti-Confederates were led by Peter Cashin, who called the deal an "unholy union" between London and Ottawa; to protest the union, anti-Confederates raised black flags and wore black armbands of disapproval on April 1, 1949.

To this day, conspiracy theorists contend Newfoundlanders were duped, and that in order to ensure Joey's Confederation dream, the vote results were switched and that majority "yes" votes were actually "no." Many people believe that federal jurisdiction over important industries such as fishing and offshore oil has inhibited the province's ability to manage its own affairs. Newfoundland's main source of pre-1949 revenue — customs duties — also fell under federal jurisdiction, while the financially hefty responsibilities of health care, social services, and education were given to the province.

Did you know...

that former Premier Brian Tobin earned the nickname 'Captain Canada' for his pro-Canada stance during the 1995 Quebec referendum?

They Said It

"Hurrah for our own native Isle, Newfoundland,
Not a stranger shall hold one inch of its strand,
Her face turns to Britain, her back to the Gulf,
Come near at your peril, Canadian Wolf."

— **Anti-Confederate song, 1869.**

POLITICAL GEOGRAPHY

Unlike other provinces, Newfoundland and Labrador has no counties. Instead, the province is divided into four regions: Eastern, Central, Western, and Labrador; sometimes the Avalon Peninsula is considered a region by itself.

- Number of cities: 3; St. John's, Corner Brook, and Mount Pearl.
- Number of incorporated towns and rural municipalities: 282
- Number of federally recognized aboriginal communities: 15
- Number of mayors: 272
- Number of provincial ridings: 48
- Number of federal voting districts: 7
- Location of House of the Assembly: In the East Block of the Confederation Building on Prince Phillip Drive in St. John's.

Sources: Newfoundland and Labrador, Municipal Affairs; Elections Newfoundland and Labrador; Elections Canada; House of Assembly; Indian and Northern Affairs Canada.

Did you know...

that Newfoundland was originally slated to become a Canadian province on April 1? Fearful of becoming the "fools" of Canadian Confederation, the province instead opted to join Canada technically in the dying minutes of March 31. The official swearing-in and parties were delayed until April 2.

PREMIERS AND THEIR OCCUPATIONS

Premier	Party	Term	Former Occupation
Danny Williams	Progressive Conservative	2003 -	lawyer, businessman
Roger Grimes	Liberal	2001 - 2003	educator
Beaton Tulk	Liberal	2000 - 2001	educator, civil servant
Brian Tobin	Liberal	1996 - 2000	broadcaster, political aide
Clyde K. Wells	Liberal	1989 - 1996	lawyer
Thomas Rideout	Progressive Conservative	March 22 - May 5, 1989	teacher
A. Brian Peckford	Progressive Conservative	1979 - 1989	teacher
Frank D. Moores	Progressive Conservative	1972 - 1979	businessman
Joey Smallwood	Liberal	1949 - 1972	journalist, political organizer

THE CURRENT ADMINISTRATION

- Premier: The Honourable Danny Williams
- Party: Progressive Conservatives
- Date elected: October 21, 2003
- Date sworn into office: November 6, 2003
- Date re-elected: October 9, 2007
- Voter turnout in the last provincial election: 62 percent
- Number of seats in the Newfoundland and Labrador House of Assembly: 48
- Number of PC seats held: 44
- Number of Liberal seats held: 3
- Number of New Democrat seats held: 1

Source: Government of Newfoundland and Labrador.

They Said It

"I write this Introduction to her new book as a tribute to a feisty, sometimes ferocious, feminist protagonist, never shy or retiring but redoubtable political personality. She was a constant thorn in my side while she was in Opposition, but her marriage to my fellow Newfoundlander Austin Thorne has made her more serene and has calmed her sometimes volcanic and partisan excesses."

— **John Crosbie on Sheila Copps, written as the forward to Copps's autobiography, *Worth Fighting For.***

WOMEN FIRSTS IN POLITICS

1925: Earn right to vote

1957: First mayor - Dorothy Drover (Clarenville)

1973: First selected for jury duty

1974: First mayor of St. John's - Dorothy Wyatt

1975: First in House of Assembly - Hazel McIsaac

1979: First Cabinet ministers - Hazel Newhook, Lynn Verge

1983: First Supreme Court justice - Dorothy Cameron

1986: First Senator - Ethel Cochrane

1989: First Deputy Premier - Lynn Verge

1993: First elected to House of Commons - Bonnie Hickey and Jean Payne

1995: First party leader - Lynn Verge (Progressive Conservative)

2008: Percentage of women in the House of Assembly - 23.4

Source: "Guide 2 Women Leaders."

Did you know...

that when federal Finance Minister John Crosbie – now the province's Lieutenant Governor – delivered his 1979 federal budget speech, he followed the tradition of wearing new shoes? On budget day, he donned traditional Labrador footwear – mukluks!

FRANCHISE FACTS

To participate legally in Newfoundland and Labrador elections, a voter must be a Canadian citizen, at least 18 years old on polling day, and be a resident of the province the day beforehand. Voters must also, on the day of the vote, reside in the electoral district in which they cast their ballots.

Sources: Elections Newfoundland and Labrador; Heritage Newfoundland; Status of Women Canada.

Bio PREMIER DANNY WILLIAMS

Born in St. John's on August 4, 1950, into a staunch Tory family, Williams studied political science and economics at Memorial University, winning a Rhodes Scholarship in 1969. He earned a B.A. in Law at Oxford University, then a law degree from Dalhousie University. Called to the Bar in 1972, he was appointed to the Queen's Counsel in 1984.

While still in law school, Williams led a consortium that won the province's first cable-TV licence; from 1975 he helmed Cable Atlantic to great success, eventually selling the company for $280 million. His high-profile St. John's law firm represented many of the victims of sexual abuse at the city's former Mount Cashel Orphanage. Williams was also involved in the offshore petroleum industry, and in golf course and hotel ventures (thus the nickname sometimes seen in the press: Danny Millions).

From the beginning of his tenure in office, Williams took controversial positions. He started by cutting government spending and froze public-sector wages. This prompted 20,000 public employees to strike—the province legislated them back to work. Williams cut more jobs by streamlining provincial health and education boards. His government was on the way to balancing the budget, but was leaving resentment and a few bruised feelings in its wake.

Williams also took Prime Minister Paul Martin to task for a perceived broken election promise to stop clawbacks of federal equalization payments. In the heat of that dispute, the irate premier

FEDERAL POLITICS

As of yet, no residents of 24 Sussex Drive have hailed from Newfoundland and Labrador. Perhaps the closest a Newfoundlander has come to Canada's highest public office was when John Crosbie, who was popular but hampered by his inability to speak French, finished a strong third in the 1983 Progressive Conservative leadership race.

Brian Tobin's January 2006 announcement that he would not run for leader of the federal Liberals extended the length of time we will wait for a Newfoundland-born prime minister.

ordered all Canadian flags removed from provincial offices. In 2005, a deal that satisfied him—a new Atlantic Accord—was struck.

Next opponent: Big Oil. Unhappy with the royalty scheme the industry was offering for the proposed offshore Hebron Ben Nevis field, and seeking an equity stake for the province, Williams balked - and the companies walked. Many who had supported the premier in his previous dust-ups wondered if he had gone too far this time, but within a year the oil companies were back at the table and an agreement was reached.

In 2007, the provincial constituency-allowance spending scandal broke: the Auditor General accused former and current MHAs - from all parties - of overspending, inappropriate spending, and double-billing. The scandal took down, among others, the premier's right-hand man, Jerry Byrne. Williams stayed above the fray, however, deploring the dishonest activities; he gives his salary to charity, and no suspicion of wrongdoing has attached to him.

Danny Williams won his second term in October 2007, in a landslide victory that nearly obliterated the opposition. In the eyes of a substantial majority of Newfoundlanders and Labradorians, he is a principled leader whose pugnacious style reflects a widespread belief that the province has been given the short end of the stick for far too long.

FEDERAL MATH

- Newfoundlanders and Labradorians in the House of Commons: 7 out of 308 seats
- Number of Senators: 5 out of 105 seats (plus one vacancy)

Take 5 FIVE JOHN CROSBIE QUOTES

Although the recently installed (February 2008) Lieutenant-Governor brings experience and stature to the office, and is expected to conduct its affairs with dignity befitting its responsibilities, the Honourable Mr. Crosbie does have a history of shooting from the hip.

1. **"Just quiet down, baby."** Said to Sheila Copps during a parliamentary debate in 1985.
2. **"It is better to be sincere in one language than to be a twit in two."** In 1983, discussing his monolingualism and the bilingualism of Pierre Trudeau.
3. **"Pass the tequila, Sheila, and lay down and love me again."** In 1990, song lyrics Crosbie said Sheila Copps reminded him of.
4. **"Down in Newfoundland, we can hardly sleep for wondering when St. Pierre and Miquelon are going to invade."** In 1983, on the state of Canada's military.
5. **"The problem with fellow Newfoundland MLA Tom Burgess was that his support could never be bought. At best, he could be rented, and perhaps only by the hour."**

Weblinks

Office of the Premier
www.premier.gov.nl.ca/premier/
Featuring a biography, press releases and contact information, this site is your link to the office of the premier.

Progressive Conservative Party of Newfoundland and Labrador
www.pcparty.nf.net/
The official website of Danny Williams and the Progressive Conservatives.

Liberal Party of Newfoundland and Labrador
www.liberal.nf.net/
The official website of the Yvonne Jones (the acting leader) and the Liberal Party.

Newfoundland and Labrador New Democratic Party
www.nl.ndp.ca/
The official website of Lorraine Michael and the NDP.

Green Party of Canada
www.greenparty.ca
Visit Ted Warren (NL's organizer) at the official website of the Green Party of Canada.

Did you know...

that Newfoundland and Labrador is one of only three provinces in the country to set fixed election dates? Elections are held on the second Tuesday in October four years after the most recently held general election. The next general election will be held October 11, 2011.

Then and Now

Before European settlement, Newfoundland and Labrador was home to four aboriginal groups: the Beothuk and Mi'kmaq on mainland Newfoundland, the Innu of southern Labrador, and the Inuit of Northern Labrador.

Until the 1820s, Britain overtly discouraged the settlement of Newfoundland and Labrador. Europeans would travel to the region in the spring, fish through the summer, and return to Europe in the fall. Thus, the European population in Newfoundland and Labrador was very small in its early history. In 1750, an estimated 6,900 Europeans wintered in Newfoundland and of these, only 2,676 lived permanently on the Island.

POPULATION THEN AND NOW

1763:	12,000
1807:	26,500
1823:	75,000
1857:	124,288
1901:	217,037
1951:	361,416
2007:	505,469

Take 5 FIVE VIKINGS
IN NEWFOUNDLAND AND LABRADOR HISTORY

1. **Eric the Red**, colonizer of Greenland.
2. **Leif Eriksson**, Eric's son, the first European to come from Greenland to Labrador.
3. **Thorfinn Karlsefni**, the wife of a Vinland colonist.
4. **Snorri**, the son of Thorfinn Karlsefni, who was the first European born in North America.
5. **Bjarni Herjolfsson**, an Icelandic trader who, in 986, was one of the first Vikings to spy Labrador when his crew was driven off course en route to Greenland from Iceland.

BIRTH RATE PER 1,000 POPULATION

Newfoundland and Labrador		Canada
1901	7.0	31.2
1951	32.5	27.2
2007	8.6	10.5

Sources: Statistics Canada; Government of Newfoundland and Labrador; Status of Women Canada.

EARLY FOLK REMEDIES OF NEWFOUNDLAND AND LABRADOR

- To stop bleeding: Apply cobwebs.
- Warts: Rub fresh meat on the wart then bury the meat. As the meat decays the wart will disappear.
- Toothaches: Rinse mouth with vinegar.
- Pain in side: Place a pebble under the afflicted person's tongue.
- Headache: Walk backwards in a circle.

Did you know...

that "tilts," small seasonal homes along the Labrador coast, were known for their unique wallpaper? Although many residents could not read, they decorated walls with pages of newspapers and magazines.

- Boils: Apply a poultice of soap, flour and molasses.
- Stomach troubles: A tea of boiled juniper, alderberry, or dogberry extract.
- Hemorrhoids: An application of pine tar.
- Ingrown nails: Drip hot tallow from a melted candle on the affliction.
- Rheumatism: Stinky, bottled brown jelly fish is said to bring relief.
- Coughs: Elixirs of wild cherry extract, turpentine (pine tree sap) or kerosene oil mixed with molasses. Steeped snakeroot is also said to be an effective cough suppressant.

Source: Historic Newfoundland and Labrador.

EDUCATION THEN AND NOW

The first school in Newfoundland and Labrador dates from 1726. It was established at Bonavista "for all poor people" of all denominations by the Church of England's missionary organization, the Society for the Propagation of the Bible.

By the end of the 18th century there were about 30 schools in Newfoundland; they held classes from 6 am to 6 pm. By 1842, the Society operated 60 schools with 3,500 pupils. In 1836 the government of Newfoundland passed its first Education Act. For the first time, state-funded schooling was available, with costs shared by Catholic and Protestant churches. Yet by 1900, fewer than half of all children of elementary school were attending school, and educational standards were low.

In 1949, the new province's denominational education system was protected by the terms of Confederation. By 1971/72, Newfoundland

Did you know...

that between 1857 and 1949, Newfoundland issued about 300 of its own postage stamps? These stamps can still be used in Canada.

schools were at an all-time peak, with an enrolment of 162,000 pupils. In 2006/7, five school boards operated 285 public schools in Newfoundland and Labrador, and educated 74,304 students. Today, Newfoundland and Labrador boasts the lowest teacher-student ratio in Canada — each teacher has an average of 13.6 students.

Sources: Government of Newfoundland and Labrador, Department of Education; "Newfoundland History," Claude Bélanger, Marianopolis College; Heritage Newfoundland.

MEMORIAL UNIVERSITY OF NEWFOUNDLAND

- Year in which Memorial University (MUN) was founded (as Memorial University College — a living memorial to veterans of the First World War): 1925
- Year in which Memorial University was granted degree-conferring status: 1949
- Year in which it opened its modern St. John's campus: 1961
- Number of students enrolled in its first year: 307
- Number in 1950-51: 400
- Number in 1969-70: 7,289
- Number of students who study at MUN today: 17,509
- Cost of undergraduate tuition in 2005/2006: $2,550

Sources: Government of Newfoundland and Labrador; Memorial University of Newfoundland; Alice Collins, "Memorial University of Newfoundland"; Association of Universities and Colleges of Canada; MUN Fact Book 2006/07.

Did you know...

that, according to legend, Sheila NaGiera was the first European woman to settle in Newfoundland, when she and her husband Gilbert Pike made the Island their home in 1611? Gilbert was a fisherman and ex-pirate; Sheila was a member of a wealthy Irish family. As the story goes, they met and fell in love in a high-seas adventure that also involved the privateer Peter Easton, and they put down roots in Carbonear. By 1650, still only 13 percent of the European residents in Newfoundland were women.

FASTER THAN A NEWFIE BULLET

By the early 20th century, trains began to rival sailing as the dominant mode of transport in Newfoundland. Work had began on the trans-Island Newfoundland Railway in the late 1800s. In time, the Railway's passenger train would come to be affectionately known as the "Newfie Bullet" — a cheerful reference to the fact that it could take up to three days to cross the Island.

To save money, the tracks were laid to a narrow gauge. As a result, when goods were exported to the mainland, the train wheels had to be changed to accommodate the wider standard track. Although the 1949 terms of Confederation promised the maintenance of railroads in perpetuity, the railway has now been phased out, and the rail bed has become the T'Railway, a 900-km-long park.

- Year in which trains first traversed the province: 1881
- Year of the first passenger train: 1898
- Distance of the main line from St. John's to Port-aux-Basques: 882 km
- Total length of all tracks in the rail system at its peak in the early 1900s: 1,458 km
- Month and year in which train passenger service ended: July 1969
- Month and year of the last freight train: June 1988

Sources: Heritage Newfoundland; "Newfoundland History," Claude Bélanger, Marianopolis College.

Did you know...

that Edith Weeks Hooper was the first Newfoundland-born woman to become a medical doctor and the first female doctor to practice in the province? She graduated from the University of Toronto Medical School in 1906.

Holidays Then and Now

Candlemas Day: Other North Americans focus on groundhogs on February 2, but some Newfoundlanders remember the European tradition of watching if a bear, emerging from hibernation, will see his shadow — a predictor of the end of winter. "If Candlemas Day be clear and fine, the rest of winter is left behind; If Candlemas Day be rough and grum, there's more of winter left to come." Candlemas Day in the Catholic tradition celebrates the purification of Mary and the presentation of Jesus at the Temple. The celebration features the consumption of a Candlemas cake, a sweetbread.

Pancake Night: Newfoundlanders add a twist to the religious tradition of Shrove Tuesday. They bake small objects — each with a particular meaning — into their pancakes. If you find a coin cooked into your pancake, you can bank on being rich. If you find a pencil stub, chances are you will become a teacher.

St. Patrick's Day: The Monday after March 17 is a provincial holiday in Newfoundland and Labrador, a commemoration of St. Patrick and celebration of many residents' Irish heritage.

St. George's Day: This provincial holiday honouring England's patron saint lands on the Monday following April 23. In ancient Rome, St. George opposed the torture of Christians; during the Crusades, a vision of St. George is said to have assured a Norman victory.

Discovery Day: Once called Midsummer's Day, with origins in pre-Christian Europe, the June 24 holiday has become St. John's Day in the capital city. As a provincial holiday it's called Discovery Day, and traditional celebrations (especially in areas of the province with Irish heritage) include lighting bonfires.

Memorial Day: Since the end of the First World War, Newfoundlanders have commemorated July 1, 1916 — the anniversary of the Battle of the Beaumont-Hamel (the first day of the Battle of the Somme), in which hundreds of Newfoundland men lost their lives. Today, July 1 is also Canada Day; on the Sunday nearest this date, parades and memorial services are still held to remember the war dead.

Orangemen's Day: Orangemen's Day, July 12, is a provincial holiday in Newfoundland and Labrador. "The Glorious Twelfth" commemorates the date in 1690 when England's Protestant King, William of Orange, defeated the former King James, a Catholic, in the Battle of the Boyne in Ireland. By the end of the 1800s, Orangemen's Day parades, picnics and dances were common in Newfoundland.

Regatta Day: Originating in 1825, Regatta Day remains a highlight of the St. John's summer. On the first Wednesday in August (or the first fine day after that date if the Wednesday weather is bad for rowing), the city's residents assemble in the tens of thousands to watch boat races on Quidi Vidi Lake.

Thanksgiving: When Newfoundland joined Canada, Thanksgiving was not a government-recognized holiday in the new province, although the Thanksgiving sentiment was part of harvest celebrations held in the fall. Today, Newfoundland and Labrador observes Canadian Thanksgiving.

Halloween: Newfoundland and Labrador's exuberant celebration of this holiday sets it apart from other Canadian provinces. The few days before October 31 are known as "Mischief Week." During this time, children play pranks, such as soaping windows. Bonfires are also part of these celebrations, and mischievous youngsters have been known to steal old tires and derelict boats and fences to fuel them. In some places, torches fashioned out of oil-soaked boots and mops were paraded through town on Halloween.

Guy Fawkes Day: November 5 is bonfire night. The tradition's source, probably not widely remembered by the young bonfire burners, commemorates the death of Guy Fawkes, who led an attempt in 1605 to blow up England's king and members of Parliament in retaliation for the repression of Roman Catholics in England.

Advent Sunday: In Labrador, carrying on the tradition brought by Moravian missionaries, children still hang advent stockings and small advent trees and receive gifts on December 6.

Tipp's Eve: This December 23 celebration is the first of the Christmas season along the south coast of Newfoundland. This evening, also known as Tipsy Eve, calls for the consumption of the holiday season's first Christmas cheer. In outport communities, Christmas was the only time of year when people did not work, and the 12 days of Christmas were strictly observed.

St. Stephen's Day: Now known as Boxing Day, December 26 marks the beginning of Christmas mummering, though enthusiasts have been known to start the fun on Christmas Day.

New Year's Eve: December 31 not only finds Newfoundlanders and Labradorians ringing in the New Year — some also hang stockings and give gifts to mark its arrival.
Source: Heritage Newfoundland.

HITTIN' THE HIGHWAY

- Year in which the automobile made its debut: 1903
- Year in which drivers switched to right-side driving, 25 years after the last Canadian province made the change: 1947
- Year in which the Burin Peninsula highway was completed and saw its first automobile traffic: 1949
- Between 1949 and 1968, the percentage increase in the number of motor vehicles: 900
- The increase in paved roads between 1949 and 1968: 194 km to 1,868 km
- Number of km of paved road today: 6,995 km
- Percentage of roads that are paved: 78
- Length of the province's portion of the TransCanada highway: 908 km

Did you know...

that early Newfoundland "currency" consisted of dried codfish?

Did you know...

that Memorial University of Newfoundland is the largest university in Atlantic Canada?

They Said It

"Have struck iceberg."

— the message received by the Cape Race, Newfoundland, wireless station at 10:35 pm, April 4, 1912, from the doomed *Titanic*.

ELECTRICITY

Today, plugged-in Newfoundlanders and Labradorians take electricity for granted, since it fuels so many modern conveniences. It is easy to forget that this was not always the case.

- Year in which the St. John's Electric Light Company brought electricity to the province: 1885
- Year in which the St. John's Street Railway Company established the first hydroelectric plant: 1900
- In 1920, these two companies merged to form the St. John's Light and Power Company, renamed in 1924 as the Newfoundland Light and Power Company, and in 1990 as Newfoundland Power
- Approximate percentage of Newfoundlanders with electricity by Confederation in 1949: 50
- Year in which the Newfoundland and Labrador Power Commission was created, part of Smallwood's plan to electrify his province: 1954
- Year by which virtually all Newfoundlanders had electricity: 1972

Sources: Heritage Newfoundland; Melvin Baker, "Rural Electrification in Newfoundland in the 1950s and the Origins of the Newfoundland Power Commission."

TELEPHONES

St. John's got Newfoundland's first telephones in March 1878, when postmaster John Delaney installed two phones he had built using instructions from the magazine *Scientific American*. They connected Delaney's home with that of a fellow post office employee, and were used mainly for post office business.

- Year in which Archibald's Furniture in St. John's got the Island's second phones: 1884

- Year in which the first public phone system was established: 1885
- In 1921, the annual cost of a residential phone system: $30
- Year in which the first long distance line was installed: 1921
- Date on which the first long distance call was made, between Brigus and Harbour Grace: November 27, 1921
- Date on which a phone conversation between Governor Sir Humphrey Walwyn and Canadian Governor General Lord Tweedsmuir became the first phone call between Canada and Newfoundland: January 10, 1939
- Year in which Newfoundland got its first dial phone service: 1948
- Year in which cellular phone services were established: 1990

Source: Newfoundland and Labrador Department of Education.

Take 5 — NFLD AND LABRADOR'S
TOP FIVE CONTRIBUTIONS TO AVIATION HISTORY

Thanks to its location on the eastern edge of North America, Newfoundland has been involved in some important aviation milestones.

1. **First transatlantic flight:** In May 1919, an NC-4, piloted by Lieutenant Commander Albert Read, made history when it flew from Trepassey Bay to Lisbon, Portugal.
2. **First nonstop transatlantic flight:** On June 15-16, 1919, British aviators John Alcock and Arthur Whitten Brown, made the 3,041.7 km flight from Lester's Field near St. John's to Clifden, Ireland. It took 16 hours and 12 minutes.
3. **First woman's solo transatlantic flight:** On May 20, 1932, famed pilot Amelia Earhart took off from Harbour Grace and 15 hours later arrived in Ireland.
4. **First transatlantic seaplane service:** In 1939 Pan American Airways offered the world's first transatlantic seaplane service, with stops in Newfoundland.
5. **First transatlantic round trip in same day:** On August 26, 1952, a British twin-jet bomber flew from Northern Ireland to Gander and back again in 7 hours and 59 minutes.

TELEVISION

- Year in which the province's first TV station, CJON, began broadcasting: 1955
- Number of stations broadcasting by 1964: 3 (CJON, CBYT in Corner Brook and CBNT in St. John's)
- Year in which Ted Russell's "The Holdin' Ground" was the first TV drama to be filmed in Newfoundland: 1959
- Years in which Newfoundlanders faithfully tuned into CBC's "All Around the Circle," a showcase of Newfoundland entertainment: 1967-1979
- Year in which the comedy CODCO debuted on television: 1986
- Number of seasons CODCO was on the national CBC network: 5
- Year in which CBC's "Land and Sea" celebrated its 40th anniversary: 2008

MUMMERING

Mummering (or mumming or janneying) is an ancient custom enjoyed by many Newfoundlanders and Labradorians. Mummers don disguises and visit friends and family in the community, who must guess the identities of their costumed visitors.

The roots of mummering may go as far back as 6th century Rome, to a time when the Church outlawed dramatic productions and entertainers began to wander to find private audiences for their shows. The custom can certainly be traced back hundreds of years in England and Ireland. Irish immigrants brought mummering, which by then had become an annual Christmastime activity, to Newfoundland. In the 19th century Newfoundland mummers performed short dramas — today a visit by mummers is almost always far less structured.

Beginning on St. Stephen's Day, December 26, and at any time dur-

Did you know...

that in 1939, a three-minute call from St. John's to Montreal cost $7.50 and a similar call to London cost $22.20?

ing the next 12 days (until Epiphany), Newfoundlanders disguise themselves (and their voices) to visit friends and family. Hosts must offer refreshments to the unknown visitors, who have dressed in odd bits of clothing to hide their height or girth as well as their faces, and guess who they are. Each time the host fails to guess the mummer's identity, he or she may be required to give a drink (of grog) to the mummer.

Mummering was banned in 1861 following several rowdy years when the alcohol that went along with the practice ignited political tensions and violence. It survived in the outports, however, and in many places is still practised. In fact, Newfoundlanders around the world who find themselves far from home at Christmas are known to throw mummering parties.

Source: Heritage Newfoundland.

THEN COMES MARRIAGE

In the early days of European settlement, marriage was regulated by local custom. Newfoundland and Labrador were sparsely populated and clergy were few. Unencumbered by English marriage laws, anyone who could read a marriage service could officiate at a Newfoundland wedding.

In the early 1800s, concern grew over this practice. In 1817 Newfoundland's first Marriage Act was written — it stipulated that to be legal, a marriage ceremony had to be performed by an Anglican or Catholic clergyman, or a magistrate. In 1833, the year after the creation of responsible government, the Newfoundland legislature passed a new Marriage Act allowing clergy of any denomination to conduct marriages.

Source: Trudi Johnson, '"A Matter of Custom and Convenience': Marriage Law in Nineteenth Century Newfoundland."

Did you know...

that beginning in 1966, both Canada and France began issuing permits to explore for oil and gas on and around the St. Pierre Bank? The dispute of land claims was settled in 1972.

Nautical Disasters

RMS *Titanic*

On April 14, 1912, the Marconi Company Wireless station at Cape Race, Newfoundland, received a distress message from the "unsinkable" *Titanic*, the flagship of the White Star Line Steamship Company, after the vessel struck an iceberg 590 km off the coast of Newfoundland. Despite valiant efforts by ships in the area, only 705 of 2,227 on board were rescued.

Great sealing disaster

In March 1914, 78 sealers died when, because of a misunderstanding between ship captains, they were abandoned on the ice.

Viking

In 1931, a wooden ship being featured in the film production *The Viking* exploded during filming, killing the producer and 26 others.

Caribou

A German U-Boat torpedoed the *Caribou* on October 13, 1942, as the ferry was sailing from North Sydney, Nova Scotia, to Port aux Basques, Newfoundland. Of the crew of 46, mostly Newfoundlanders, 31 were lost. Fifteen-month-old Leonard Shiers was the only child of the 15 on board to survive. In Port aux Basques, the result was devastating: 21 new widows mourned their lost husbands.

The Ocean Ranger

On February 15, 1982, a vicious storm produced the worst offshore drilling disaster in Canada's history when 100-foot seas caused the giant oil rig to capsize, killing all 84 crew members.

Ryan's Commander

On September 19, 2004, the 65-foot *Ryan's Commander* capsized in heavy winds and waves off Cape Bonavista. Two of the six on board died despite a dramatic rescue attempt. Since then, the design of offshore fishing vessels — especially their ballast systems — has been called into question.

Melina and Keith II

On September 12, 2005, the *Melina and Keith II* sank off Cape Bonavista and four of the six crew drowned while waiting for rescue. One of the survivors stayed above the icy water by clinging to an overturned life raft for nearly four hours. The local media blamed rescue procedures, which gave the rescue helicopter more than two hours to get off the ground — instead of the usual 30 minutes — because the accident occurred outside regular office hours.

MARRIAGE TODAY

You must be 19 years of age to marry in Newfoundland and Labrador. Today, a marriage licence costs $50, and is valid for 30 days. An applicant must wait four days after ordering the licence before it is issued. Another four days must pass after it is issued before the officiant can conduct the marriage. On December 21, 2004, Newfoundland and Labrador began issuing marriage licences to same-sex couples.

Source: Government of Newfoundland and Labrador.

Take 5 GERALD SQUIRES'S TOP FIVE
FAVOURITE MEMORIES OF HIS EXPLOITS ISLAND CHILDHOOD

Artist Gerald Squires, whose paintings of the province's landscapes also reveal much of its psyche, was born in 1937 in Change Islands and grew up there and on Exploits Island. A Member of the Order of Canada who has been highly honoured for his work, he now lives and paints in Holyrood and operates a gallery in St. John's.

1. **The landwash where I went "paddling"**—walking in the water by the shore, but only out as far as short "long rubbers" would allow.

2. **"Copy pans"** in the spring, jumping from one pan of ice to another, killing imaginary seals.

3. **The massive rock face behind the well house where we would play and hide in the caves**, and pretend to be anyone other than who we were.

4. How you could see the devil's cloven foot imprinted on the **"Kissing Rock"** on a moonlit night, coming home late from Sunday night service at the Salvation Army Hall.

5. **Watching my neighbour, Flossie Millie**, make what I thought to be a perfect drawing of the *Clyde*, the coastal vessel, as she first docked after the ice breakup in the spring.

Did you know...

that in 1961 Bob Hope performed in Labrador at the Goose Bay Air Force Base, and in Newfoundland at Argentia and at Harmon AFB in Stephenville, all American military bases? Many other celebrities, including Elvis Presley, Marilyn Monroe and Frank Sinatra performed at bases in the province.

PUB POPULARITY

Newfoundland and Labrador, and St. John's in particular, have a reputation for their revelry. Pubs and bars were part of the earliest European landscape in Newfoundland. In 1726 there were just 450 families living in Newfoundland — but they kept 65 public houses. That same year, the new town of St. John's had 42 homes ... and 16 taverns! Today there are approximately 600 bars in the province, which generate at least $10 million in sales each year.

Sources: The Independent; Michael Harris, Rare Ambition: The Crosbies of Newfoundland.

NORTHERN COD, THEN AND NOW

On June 2, 1992, the federal government declared a moratorium on the Northern Cod fishery, effectively putting 19,000 fishers and plant workers and 20,000 others out of work. The cod fishery has never rebounded,

Did you know...

that Newfoundlanders and Labradorians are the Canadians least likely to head for divorce court?

Did you know...

that Newfoundland's first commercial radio station, VOGY, hit the airwaves on September 12, 1932? It broadcast from a studio in St. John's' posh Crosbie Hotel.

and its dismal state stands in sharp contrast to its glory years.

The Vikings were the first Europeans to use cod as their main source of food, during their brief time in Newfoundland around 1000. Nearly 500 years later, John Cabot's observation that "the schools of cod in the waters off Newfoundland were so thick that they slowed the ship," set off a veritable 'cod-rush' in fish-hungry Europe. The cod catch seemed to know no bounds; in 1962, 1.6 million tonnes of the fish spawned off Newfoundland and Labrador and six years later an all-time record 810,000 tonnes were caught.

In 1977, Canada secured an exclusive 320 km fishing limit off its east coast. Before this time, any Canadian or foreign vessel could fish virtually anywhere off the coast. By 1985 inshore fishers had concerns about declining cod stocks. In 1992, there were just 22,000 tonnes of the fish spawning off the coast, prompting Ottawa to take the "temporary" step of closing the fishery.

Limited local fisheries were conducted between 1998 to 2002, and again in 2006 and 2007, to assess the cod stocks, which some fishermen claimed were on the increase. It appears populations have rebounded in certain inshore areas; the overall stocks, however, remain at a low level — particularly offshore — and scientists are not optimistic that they will recover.

Sources: Heritage Newfoundland; "Between The Rock and a Hard Place: The Destruction of Newfoundland's Outport Communities"; Electronic Green Journal, "The Newfoundland Cod Stock Collapse: A Review and Analysis of Social Factors."

Weblinks

Railway Society of Newfoundland
www.durham.net/~kburt/NewfoundlandTrains.html
Find out more about the railways that used to criss-cross the province.

Animated History
www.epe.lac-bac.gc.ca/100/205/301/ic/cdc/rock/default.htm
Great for kids of all ages, this website uses flash animation to tell visitors about the history of Newfoundland and Labrador.

Newfoundland Resettlement
www.mun.ca/mha/resettlement/rs_intro.php
Newfoundland resettlement has, to a considerable extent, defined the experiences of Newfoundlanders in the 20th century. Learn all about it here.

Newfoundland and Labrador Heritage
www.heritage.nf.ca/home.html
An excellent place to learn more about the province's history and heritage.

First People

TIMELINE

9000 BP (Before Present): The first inhabitants, probably descendants of Paleo-Indians (who were the first to arrive in North America from Asia), move into southern Labrador after giant ice sheets recede.

7500 BP: These settlers develop a unique culture centred on the sea. Considered today to have belonged to the Maritime Archaic tradition, they flourish for several thousand years.

5000 BP: These Maritime Archaic people begin to inhabit the island of Newfoundland.

4000-3000 BP: A new people, called Paleo-Eskimos, reach northern Labrador, and before 3000 BP reach the Island.

3000 BP: For reasons unknown, the Maritime Archaic people disappear.

3500-2000 BP: Another group, the Intermediate People (possibly descended from Maritime Archaic people), users of new types of tools, inhabit interior Labrador.

3000 BP: The population of Newfoundland and Labrador grows rapidly with a new culture now referred to as the Groswater People. Related to the Paleo-Eskimo, they will disappear from Newfoundland by 2200 BP, and from Labrador shortly afterward.

2800 BP: A culture identifiable as Dorset Paleo-Eskimo inhabits coastal Labrador and the Northern Peninsula of Newfoundland.

2000-800 BP: The Recent Indian people form settlements in Newfoundland and Labrador. In Newfoundland, they are considered to be the direct ancestors of the Beothuk, and in Labrador of the Innu.

1000 BP: The last of the Paleo-Eskimo disappear from the Island; within a few centuries, they are gone from Labrador, too.

700-800 BP: The earliest Thule, believed to be ancestors of today's Labrador Inuit, inhabit northern Labrador.

400 BP: Historical evidence confirms the presence of the Mi'kmaq in Newfoundland and Labrador.

FIRST PEOPLE TODAY

Newfoundland and Labrador is home to four First Nations groups: the Inuit, the Innu, the Mi'kmaq, and the Métis.

- Number of Aboriginal people in Canada: 1,172,790
- Number in Newfoundland and Labrador: 23,450
- Percentage of Canadian Aboriginals who live in Newfoundland and Labrador: 1.99
- Number of Newfoundlanders and Labradorians whose mother tongue is an Aboriginal language: 2,185
- Number of Aboriginal people who live in St. John's: 2,015

Sources: Statistics Canada; Heritage Newfoundland.

THE BEOTHUK

One of the most tragic stories in Newfoundland and Labrador's history is the loss of an entire Aboriginal people, the Beothuk. A creation story attributed to the Beothuk tells of how they sprang from an arrow stuck in the ground; it is doubtful that early Beothuk storytellers could possibly have foretold their demise. By 1829 there were no Beothuk left in Newfoundland, though residents have stories of half-blood ancestors.

BEOTHUK CULTURE

As part of the Algonkian family, the Beothuk probably numbered around 700 people at the time of first European contact. The Beothuk had an animistic worldview — they believed that animate and inanimate objects had spiritual dimensions. For the Beothuk, the most important spirits were the sun and moon.

THE "RED INDIANS"

European fishers who encountered the Beothuk in the 16th century commented on their use of ochre, a red pigment, to colour their skin. In subsequent years "Red Indian" was applied to many First Peoples in North America, even when it did not apply. Red ochre had important cultural meanings for the Beothuk. They covered their bodies, clothes, weapons, utensils, canoes and even their infants with the pigment to symbolize their tribal identity. The name "Beothuk" comes from the people's own name for themselves — "Beathook" and "Behathook," which translates as "Red Indian."

Did you know...

that one of the best places to learn about the Beothuk is at the Boyd's Cove Interpretation Centre? The provincial historic site is situated near one of the last known Beothuk seasonal encampments on the Exploits River.

AND THEN COMES EUROPE

Early European settlement in Newfoundland was largely migratory, with fishers remaining just for the fishing season. Instead of trading with the Europeans, the Beothuk picked up metal scraps they left behind, fashioning them into a wide range of tools, such as harpoon blades, awls and arrowheads.

Because the Beothuk could obtain metal this way, while other con-

Take 5 — BERT ALEXANDER'S TOP FIVE
MOST SIGNIFICANT DATES IN NEWFOUNDLAND AND LABRADOR FIRST NATIONS HISTORY

Born in Auguathuna, on the Port au Port Peninsula, to parents of Mi'kmaq ancestry, Bert Alexander lives in Kippens, on the west coast of Newfoundland. An educator, writer and aboriginal activist, he is chief of the 7,500 member Ktaqamkuk Mi'kmaq Alliance. He has long fought for equality and justice for the Mi'kmaq people of the province.

1. **1725 to 1779:** The Maritime Peace and Friendship Treaties were signed in Eastern Canada. These were designed to formalize military alliances with the First Nations, but did not involve land surrenders. First Nations people were promised by the English Crown that they could continue to hunt, fish and follow their customs and religious practices. These rights have recently been upheld by the Supreme Court of Canada in a landmark case. In Eastern Canada, the case has reopened the question of Aboriginal rights to land and coastal resources, possibly including offshore petroleum and minerals.

2. **1822:** William Cormack's expedition crossed Newfoundland. He was the first white man to traverse the Island; his guide was Sylvester Joe, a Mi'kmaq. From the top of Steel Mountain, near the town of St. Georges, you can see the location where Cormack completed his journey.

tinental Aboriginals had to trade for it, they had no need to interact with fishers. They took materials that were apparently abandoned; the fishing crews that returned each year, however, saw it as theft.

The beginning of the end arrived for the Beothuk when European settlement became permanent. The Beothuk retreated to the interior, avoiding Europeans as much as possible. For a time, Newfoundland's size and rich resources meant there were buffer zones between the Beothuk and the Europeans, but as settlement increased they began to disappear.

3. **April 1, 1949:** Newfoundland becomes a province of Canada. This union resulted in an agreement between the province of Newfoundland and Canada whereby the assimilation of the Mi'kmaq people of Newfoundland into the mainstream population was, in effect, legalized.

4. **1987:** The community of Conne River was registered under the Federal Indian Act as an Indian reserve. This occurred three years after the Miawpukek First Nations became registered as a band. This event was significant for those Mi'kmaq living outside of Conne River because it would establish a basis for their struggle for equality and justice.

5. **July 29, 2003:** A class-action lawsuit was filed in the Supreme Court of Newfoundland and Labrador against the federal and provincial governments on behalf of the majority of Mi'kmaq people in the province living outside of Conne River. Plaintiffs for the suit were Jake Davis, Chief of the Sip'kop Mi'kmaq Indian Band of St. Alban's, Bert Alexander, Chief of the Ktaqamkuk Mi'kmaq Alliance, and John Oliver, also a member of the Ktaqamkuk Mi'kmaq Alliance. The lawsuit seeks equality for the plaintiffs with Conne River and other First Nations peoples across Canada.

> *". . . his eyes flashed fire and he uttered a yell that made the woods echo."*
> — a witness describing the death of Nonosabasut at John Peyton's trial before a Grand Jury. Peyton was acquitted of murder.

CLOSER RELATIONSHIP TURNS DEADLY

With increased European settlement, the Beothuk faced starvation; they lost access to the coastal resources on which they relied, and faced competition for them. It became more and more difficult for them to avoid Europeans, and violence escalated. As with Aboriginal people elsewhere, the Beothuk also sickened from European diseases to which they had little immunity. Meanwhile, fishers and trappers wanted restitution for Beothuk pilfering of their fishing stations, and violent clashes did see Beothuks felled by settlers' bullets.

A MATTER OF POLICY

By 1800, European settlers had still not established a friendly relationship with the shrinking population of Beothuk. Motivated by humanitarian interests and by a desire to institute trade, the English launched a concerted campaign to find and befriend the Beothuk. Rewards were offered to anyone who brought a living Beothuk to St. John's. The plan was to treat the hostage kindly, shower him or her with presents, and then return the captive to the Beothuk, thus demonstrating kindness and goodwill.

In 1811, an English expedition sent by Governor John Duckworth met with Beothuk at Red Indian Lake, where they shared a meal. Pleased by the peaceful exchange, expedition leader Lt. David Buchan left two of his men with the Beothuk and returned to his camp to fetch presents for his hosts. The Beothuk, probably fearing Buchanan would return with more men and take them hostage, killed the two Englishmen and retreated to the woods.

MARY MARCH

Eight years after the killings at Red Indian Lake, John Peyton, Jr., angry that a boat loaded with his fishing equipment had been set adrift by the Beothuk, went after the perpetrators. When he came across a Beothuk camp, he kidnapped Demasduit, a new mother too weak to escape. When Desmasduit's husband, Nonosabasut, tried to rescue his wife and child, he was killed.

Dubbed "Mary March" by her captors (for the month in which she was taken), Demasduit was taken to Twillingate where she lived with the Reverend John Leigh. Her infant child died just two days after her capture. In mere months, her body wracked with tuberculosis, Demasduit followed her husband and child to the grave. In January 1820, her body was returned to the Beothuk, left on the spot from which she had been captured.

LAST OF THE BEOTHUK

A number of Beothuk witnessed the murder of Nonosabasut, including his young niece, Shanawdithit. Several years later, following the very hard winter of 1823-24, Shanawdithit, her mother and her sister, all sick and near starvation, threw themselves on the mercy of fur trappers. Shortly thereafter, Shanawdithit's mother and sister died.

Shanawdithit was placed in the home of the local magistrate, John Peyton, Jr. — the same man who had captured Demasduit. Shanawdithit was treated kindly, and she lived in Peyton's household for five years. A group of concerned citizens sponsored her to visit St. John's, where she was interviewed by William Cormack, the philanthropist president of the Beothuk Institute, an organization mandated to preserve the Beothuk.

Did you know...

that by the early 1800s, according to Shanawdithit, the Beothuk cultural code dictated that those who made peace with settlers were to be sacrificed to the spirits of kin slain by Europeans?

Shanawdithit provided Cormack with valuable information about her people and their culture. A gifted artist, her sketches remain one of the most important first-hand sources of knowledge about the Beothuk. Shanawdithit lived in St. John's for five years. By 1829, she was in very poor health and in June she died of tuberculosis at the age of 28. Unlike Demasduit, Shanawdithit had no family to whom she could be returned; she was buried in a grave in St. John's.

A BEOTHUK DICTIONARY

Shanawdithit left a priceless legacy: virtually everything we know of Beothuk culture, as it existed in the early 19th century, came from her. Especially important was the "dictionary" she helped William Cormack compile.

Abideeshook: domestic cat
Adothe / odeothyke: boat, vessel
Agamet: buttons, money
Beathook: Red Indian
Beteok: good night
Bukashman / bookshimon: man
Ebanthoo: water
Giwashuwet: bear
Memet: hand
Moosin / gei-je-bursut: ankle
Shedbasing: upper arm
Shegamik: to blow the nose
Stiocena: thumb
Tapaithook: canoe
Washeu: night, darkness
Weshemesh: herring
Woodrut: fire
Zatrook: husband

Source: W. E. Cormack's manuscript.

They Said It

"The situation of the unfortunate Beothuk carries with it our warmest sympathy and loudly calls on us all to do something for the sake of humanity. For my own satisfaction, I have for a time, released myself from all other avocations, and am here now, on my way to visit that part of the country which the surviving remnant of the tribe have of late years frequented, to endeavour to force a friendly interview with some of them, before they are entirely annihilated: but it will most probably require many such interviews, and some years, to reconcile them to the approaches of civilized man."

— W.E. Cormack's November 1827 statement on the establishment of the Beothuk Institute. The organization was revived in 1997 as the Beothuk Institute to develop a better awareness of the lost people.

THE INUIT OF LABRADOR

An Arctic people, the Inuit of Labrador now have their own ethnic regional government in the northern part of the province. Nunatsiavut (meaning "beautiful land") was officially created on December 1, 2005, following years of land-claims negotiations. It encompasses 72,500 km^2.

- Language: Inuktitut
- "Inuit" means "the people" in Inuktitut
- How they lived then: Before encountering Europeans, the Inuit lived by hunting and fishing. On land, caribou was the most important prey; the sea offered a harvest of seals to whales and cod to salmon throughout the year.

Did you know...

that the land-claims agreement that led to the creation of Nunatsiavut was the final such agreement to be made in Canada covering Inuit people?

- Dwellings: The Inuit had three types of traditional dwellings. In summer they lived in conical tents made of skins. On hunting trips, they built temporary snow homes. In winter, semi-permanent homes of stone and sod were dug into the ground for insulation. The Inuit burned seal oil for light and heat.
- Number of Inuit communities recognized by the federal Department of Indian and Northern Development: 5
- Contemporary Inuit: Today, many Inuit still live off the land, hunting, fishing and trapping when they can, though they may live in established communities in the winter. They also find employment in the mines of Labrador and in other non-traditional jobs.
- Population: 5,300. Inuit make up 89 percent of the population of Nunatsiavut.

Sources: Virtual Museum of Labrador, Indian and Northern Affairs Canada, Nunatsiavut Government, and Statistics Canada.

WHERE THEY LIVE
- Most Labrador Inuit live in the communities of Nain, Hopedale, Makkovik, Postville and Rigolet. In all, 4 percent of Canadian Inuit live in Labrador.
- The Inuit are the youngest aboriginals in Canada. In 2006 their median age was 22, compared with 40 for non-aboriginal Canadians. More than half (56 percent) of all Inuit are 24 or younger.

Source: Statistics Canada.

GOOD DOG!
Inuit dogs were no mere pets. They were partners in hunting. Dog teams provided transportation and assisted in the tracking and killing of game. In addition, dogs were themselves an important emergency source of food in times of extreme hardship.

INUIT SPIRITUALITY

The Inuit, like many First Peoples, believe in the power of shamans, or *angakut*. Spirit helpers, called *Torngat*, aid the shamans. The Inuit believe that all prominent geographic forms have a spiritual counterpart. The environment teems with spirits whom the Inuit have to placate or guard against. For example, to earn the favour of the spirits and ensure a successful hunt, they must place new seal skins on their kayaks, observe a taboo against chopping wood, refrain from sewing and from eating berries, and avoid the use of artificial light.

The most spiritual of Inuit sites is Torngait, on the northern Labrador coast. It is there that the Great Spirit Torngarsoak, who controls the life of all sea animals, lives in the form of a giant polar bear. Torngait is dangerous, and the Inuit take precautions when they travel there.

NUNATSIAVUT

For nearly three decades, the Inuit of Newfoundland and Labrador campaigned for recognition of, and rights in, a northern Labrador territory. In May 2004, 76.4 percent of Inuit voters cast ballots in favour of the Labrador Inuit Land Claims Agreement.

Later that year, the Labrador Inuit Land Claims Agreement Act was passed. Early in 2005, a tax agreement completed the deal. The Agreement clarifies land ownership and resource use, and allows the Inuit to develop their own economic development policies in the region's 72,500 km^2 area.

The deal also provides a measure of self-government; the Inuit government of the territory can make laws pertaining to culture and language, education, health, social services, and the administration of Inuit law in the territory's five Inuit communities.

Did you know...

that Nain, with a population of about 1,000, is the largest Inuit community in Labrador?

IN THE IMAGE OF MAN

The inukshuk, featured on the flag of Nunatsiavut, has become one of the symbols of Canada — the 2010 Vancouver Olympic Games has adopted the image as its logo. In the north, the inukshuk (which means "in the image of man") serves a practical purpose. These life-like figures built of rocks provide geographic markers on the treeless terrain of the north, the longer arm pointing in the direction one should take.

The figures can also indicate valuable hunting or fishing grounds and, in the case of larger statues, provide hunters with a place to conceal themselves from their intended prey. Inukshuks that look more like a pile of rocks rather than a human figure can contain a cache of food to sustain weary hunters.

Symbolically, these structures denote human cooperation. The rocks balance together, each supporting the other; this is a metaphor for how the Inuit view their lives and responsibilities.

THE INNU

Before encountering Europeans, the Innu migrated seasonally to take advantage of the best hunting. They had a meat-rich diet, caribou being an important staple. The taking of a caribou was often celebrated with a special feast called Mokushan.

- Home territory: Nitassinan
- What they call themselves: Innu, "human beings"

They Said It

"Most of all, being on the land reinforces the sense of belonging to the land, of being people of the land and ocean. The women say that if they are away from being on the land for too long, Inuit lose their sense of who they are."

— T. Williamson, *From Sina to Sikujâ luk: Our Footprint. Mapping Inuit Environmental Knowledge in the Nain District of Northern Labrador.*

- Language: Innu-aimun
- Dwellings: Before they built houses, the Innu lived in teepees covered in caribou skins and carpeted with the boughs of young spruce. Fires lit in the centre of the dwelling provided a source of heat and light.
- Number of Innu communities: 2
- Contemporary Innu: Today, most Innu live in one of two Labrador communities: Sheshatshiu on Lake Melville and Natuashish on the northern coast. They consider themselves part of the Innu Nation, which includes the Innu people of Quebec.
- Population: 1,550

Sources: Newfoundland and Labrador Heritage, Statistics Canada.

ORIGIN OF THE INNU HOMELAND

The Innu believe they originated in Tshishtashkamuk, a spirit world that, like their physical world, contains vegetation, water and mountains. They believe they were forced out of this world by a flood, crossing a land bridge into the real world they now inhabit.

INNU SPIRITUALITY

The Innu see their environment as a world where spirits exist and influence life. Animals have spirits and each species is ruled over by an "animal master," those of caribou and sea animals being most powerful. Others inhabitants of the Innu spirit world include giants, weather spirits and cannibals.

CARIBOU MAN

An important Innu *atanukana*, or creation story, involves Caribou Man and explains the origin of the caribou. According to the story, an Innu man went to live with a herd of caribou. When he married a female caribou, he was transformed into one of the animals and became the Caribou Master. He provides all Innu with caribou.

SHAKING TENT

Kushapatshikan, the shaking tent ritual, is one of the most important Innu traditions. It allows Innu hunters to ensure success by communicating with Caribou Man and other animal masters. During this séance-like ritual, a shaman enters a conical tent, which allows him contact with the spirit world.

Sometimes the shaman has to battle against spirits or the souls of other Innu groups; during this struggle the tent may shake furiously, greatly amusing observers. Shaking tent battles can be dangerous — those without sufficient power, accumulated by years of hunting, may even be killed.

IN SEARCH OF A HOME

In 1967 the federal government relocated 100 Mushuau Innu to the island community of Davis Inlet, a community six km away from their former village with a better harbour. In Utshimassits, or the "place of the boss," the once mobile new occupants were supposed to ease into an Ottawa-funded life of permanent and modern fixed settlement.

Sadly, the hope that was in the air on moving day faded. The bored and uprooted people of Davis Inlet were crammed into small houses that lacked basic amenities such as running water and electricity. In a community affected by high levels of unemployment, alcoholism became a serious social problem. In the 1990s, national evening newscasts brought the Davis Inlet truth to Canadians who watched children, high on solvents, proclaim that they wanted to die.

An international Native rights organization called the Davis Inlet inhabitants "the most suicide-ridden people of the world" and blamed Ottawa for their fate. Spurred by all the disheartening events, Innu elders desperate to renew their community advocated moving again, to a traditional Innu gathering place near the caribou hunting grounds.

In 2002-03, after a decade-long wait, 150 families from Davis Inlet were moved to the new location, called Natuashish. For the first time — 35 years after they were originally promised — the Innu enjoyed homes with running water and electricity. Unfortunately, many of the old problems followed the Innu to Natuashish. Alcohol abuse continues to plague the town, and family violence has emerged as a pressing concern. A Healing Strategy is being funded federally, a holistic program aimed at combating the root problems in the community and providing support for effective long-term solutions.

NATUASHISH BY THE NUMBERS

- Total registered population (2006): 658
- Percentage men: 46
- Percentage women: 54
- Total cost of construction and relocation: $165 million
- Cost of each home: $150,000

Source: CBC.

MOKUSHAN

The Innu continue to work to strengthen their culture: central to their efforts are semi-annual camp gatherings. Here elders participate in private and public *mokushans*, where they consume sacred caribou fat and bone marrow in homage to the important animal. They also discuss issues such as health and education that affect their community.

Did you know...

that in February 2008, the town of Natuashish narrowly voted to ban alcohol, in the hopes of getting continuing substance-abuse issues under control?

Did you know...

that the Métis of Labrador also consider themselves a people and are advocating for official recognition? Of mixed settler and aboriginal heritage, they live mainly in the Lake Melville area of Labrador, and on the southern coast.

MI'KMAQ

- Home territory: All of Mi'kmaq territory is known as Mi'kma'ki and the Newfoundland and Labrador part of that territory is called Ktaqamkuk
- What they call themselves: Lnu'k, "the people"
- Language: Míkmawísimk
- The Mi'kmaq traditionally spent part of the year inland hunting game, and other times along the coast fishing and hunting seals.
- Dwellings: Conical dwellings, covered in birch bark and skin, called wigwams.
- Number of federally-recognized Mi'kmaq reserves in Newfoundland and Labrador: 1 (Miawpukwek, or Conne River First Nation)
- Contemporary Mi'kmaq: 2,642 Mi'kmaq are registered at Miawpukek, but only 792 call it home. The Federation of Newfoundland Indians represents an additional 10,500 people of Mi'kmaq descent.

Source: Department of Indian Affairs and Northern Development.

A STORY OF AN ISLAND

The Mi'kmaq of Newfoundland and Labrador have a story explaining the creation of the island of Newfoundland. When the Great Spirit, Manitou, was creating the North American continent, he had extra material — rocks, swamps and trees. He threw this aside, tossing it into the sea to the northeast. Manitou called this pile of rocks, swamps and trees Wee-soc-kadao — and so the island of Newfoundland came to be.

MI'KMAQ ORIGINS ON NEWFOUNDLAND AND LABRADOR

Mi'kmaq oral tradition holds that they have lived on the island of Newfoundland permanently since before the arrival of Europeans. Others contend that although the Mi'kmaq occasionally journeyed to Newfoundland to fish and hunt, they did not live there permanently until the 1760s, when their harsh treatment at the hands of the British in Nova Scotia led many of them to relocate to Newfoundland, a region under lighter British control.

DISPLACED

The last spike in the trans-Newfoundland railway signalled progress to many in the Colony, but for the Mi'kmaq it heralded the end of a traditional way of life. When the railroad was completed in 1898, it opened up the interior to white hunters. After 1905, loggers hunting caribou in the massive area given to the pulpwood mill in Grand Falls also contributed to the animal's population decline, and by 1930 this mainstay of the Mi'kmaq diet had been hunted to near extinction.

Source: Newfoundland and Labrador Heritage.

Weblinks

Torngat Mountains National Park Reserve

www.parcscanada.pch.gc.ca/pn-np/nl/torngats/index_e.asp
All about the National Park Reserve — what's new, visitor information, natural wonders & cultural treasures, activities, learning experiences, and park management.

Innu Stories from the Land

www.tipatshimuna.ca/index.php
Find a wide range of information concerning the Innu — their history, elders' stories, contemporary endeavours, art and more.

The Mi'kmaq People of Newfoundland

www.nlmikmaq.com
A celebration of Newfoundland Mi'kmaq culture and heritage in words and images, plus information about current events.

Take Five More

As you can probably tell, we are partial to things you can count on one hand. This fun, entertaining and insightful chapter offers more interesting information about the province, straight from some of our favorite sons and daughters. Our 'informants,' famous and not so famous, were literally bursting at the seams with opinions about their province.

TAKE 5: ANGELA ANTLE'S TOP 5 ARTS NEWFOUNDLAND DESTINATIONS

Angela Antle is an artist and the host/producer of CBC Radio's "Weekend Arts Magazine" — a weekly show about "Our Galoot of a Culture" here in Newfoundland and Labrador.

1. **The House Museum, 23 Mill Road, Gillams:** This artist's studio in the idyllic Bay of Islands is an ever-changing contemporary art installation that's open to the public from July 1 to August 30 every year. Owner/artist Robyn Love also sells Wee Ball Yarns — hand-spun wool from the area coloured with natural dyes.

2. **King's Point Pottery and Craft Shop, 27 Bayside Drive, King's Point:** This funky and inviting artists' shop and studio stands out in the quiet central Newfoundland community of King's Point. Dolphins and whales have also been known to come close by to try to catch a peek of the latest ceramic works by Linda Yates and David Hayashida.

3. **Norton's Cove Studio, Main Street, Bonavista:** Printmaker Janet Davis has refurbished a local general store built by J. Kean in 1890. This charming waterside building now houses Janet's printing press and is the home of Norton's Cove cards and mini-prints.

4. **Paterson Woodworking studio and gallery, Upper Amherst Cove:** look for the lovely refurbished church with windows and doors lovingly restored by Mike Paterson. His furniture celebrates the strength and grace of traditional outport furniture. There are chairs, beds, tables, and sideboards that'll make you want to refurnish your whole house.

5. **Luben Boykov's Garden Studio and Foundry, Cadigan's Lane, Logy Bay:** Just outside St. John's in a park-like setting, there's a bronze foundry and sculpture garden with work by internationally known artist Luben Boykov. Call ahead to visit — you may get a chance to see the lost-wax process of bronze-making in process.

TAKE 5: ROARY MACPHERSON'S TOP FIVE WAYS TO EAT SALT FISH
Award winning chef Roary MacPherson completed his Chef-de-Cuisine certification at the Southern Alberta Institute of Technology. He has worked for the Fairmont Hotels in Algonquin, Kananaskis, Edmonton, and now works in his hometown of St. John's, Newfoundland.

1. **Fish and brewis:** A traditional Newfoundland dish with onions, salt fish and hard tack (bread). We also put Mount Scio savory with it for a truly Newfoundland taste.

2. **Fish cakes:** Made with potato, onion, Mount Scio savory and boiled salt fish.

3. **Boiled salt fish with scrunchions and onions:** Just ensure to change the water so that it's not too salty. It's served with a slice of bread.

4. **Salt cod fritters:** Deep fried in a batter with cocktail sauce.

5. **Salt cod au gratin:** Mix a little salt cod with a regular cod au gratin; this makes a special treat.

TAKE 5: KELLY RUSSELL'S TOP FIVE JIGS AND REELS

Kelly Russell is a renowned fiddler, multi-instrumentalist, folk-music collector, music teacher, recording and events producer, storyteller and veteran of pioneering bands Figgy Duff, Wonderful Grand Band, The Planks and The Irish Descendants. Kelly performs the authentic Newfoundland music of legendary fiddlers Rufus Guinchard & Emile Benoit and the classic "Tales of Pigeon Inlet" by his father, Ted Russell. Music notation for these tunes, along with hundreds of others, may be found in the book *Kelly Russell's Collection: The Fiddle Music of Newfoundland & Labrador — Volumes 1 & 2*.

1. **Mussels in the Corner:** Every Newfoundlander, whether a musician or not, knows this tune. It's the first tune I teach my fiddle students as it's relatively simple.

2. **Centennial Highway Reel:** My top fve must include this original composition from the legendary Rufus Guinchard. It was the first tune of his that I learned from a tape I had of his playing. When we first met in 1976, I introduced myself, took out my fiddle and played it for him. It began a very special friendship.

3. **Emile's Dream:** I must also include this jig from the late, great French Newfoundland fiddler, Emile Benoit, which he composed in his sleep. He woke up and telephoned his sister in the middle of the night who tape recorded it it over the phone so he wouldn't forget it. We are very fortunate because it is a beautiful tune.

4. **The Old Man and The Old Woman:** This traditional reel, author unknown, was the tune most favoured by step dancers years ago. If you want to get them on the floor, even today, I recommend that this tune be played.

5. **Before & After Tune:** My top five would not be complete without a tune from Labrador. Perhaps my most intriguing "discovery" as a fiddle music collector was an Inuit fiddler named Little Joe Palliser from Rigolet, Labrador. He played many rare tunes, including this one, which I have never heard elsewhere.

TAKE 5: STAN COOK'S TOP FIVE PLACES TO KAYAK

Stan Cook joined his father full-time in the family's adventure business in 1994. Stan Cook Adventure Tours, in business since 1970, specializes in soft adventure experiences and interpretive guided walks along the East Coast Trail. Cook is a former chair of the Tourism Industry Association of NL, Hospitality Newfoundland and Labrador, and is the founding chair of the Adventure Tourism Association of NL.

1. **Cape Broyle, Avalon Peninsula:** The reason why we set up our business here was because of its access, by kayak, to 14 caves, four arches, alongside dozens of sea stacks, and underneath waterfalls dropping off cliffs hundreds of feet above. That it is an extremely sheltered eight km fjord-like harbour, with whales almost daily from mid-May to September and the occasional iceberg in the Spring, makes it all the better.

2. **Great Island to La Manche:** Kayaking around the last two islands in the Witless Bay Bird Ecological Reserve is a feast for the senses. Millions of sea birds fly overhead, swim by or nest on these islands. The whale traffic there is also incredible. There are caves, arches, sea stacks, sheltered lagoons. Just don't look up with your mouth open while admiring the birds overhead.

3. **Ireland's Eye, Trinity Bay:** This beautiful paddle from the north shore of Random Island, Smith Sound, to the abandoned island community of Ireland's Eye features old houses and graveyard ruins. Great cliffs and unique protected harbours abound, as do whales and icebergs.

4. **Cottlesville to Exploits Island, Notre Dame Bay:** From sheltered paddling to open water, icebergs, shorelines, islands, abandoned communities, and Beothuk artifacts mark your route. Every kind of paddling is found in this region.

5. **Bay du Nord:** This is an incredible white-water canoe or kayak river with varied scenery and river characteristics. The wildlife is amazing and as a wilderness trip it is first class, although certain spots can be tricky and even dangerous. In 1982, my father left a couple of his teeth behind when he became swamped as he led a small group down this river.

TAKE 5: DEE MURPHY'S TOP FIVE SPORTS IDOLS

Dee Murphy has been involved with the sports media in Newfoundland and Labrador for more than 50 years. He has written for four publications and appeared on more than a thousand local programs discussing and reporting sporting news. Murphy has played softball, soccer, baseball, bowling, table tennis, broom ball, and is a past member of the Royal Newfoundland Regatta Committee. He is an inductee into the Canadian Softball Hall of Fame and the Newfoundland and Labrador Sports Hall of Fame. He is currently writing a book about sports heroes in Newfoundland and Labrador history.

1. **Top team:** The Brad Gushue Rink. The team took home Olympic gold for curling at the 2006 Turin Olympic Games.

2. **Top male:** Ted Gillies. An all around althlete, he played hockey, baseball, soccer, was a track star and once filled in for another bowler and scored 800.

3. **Top female:** Marg Davis. She played ice, ball and field hockey, as well as soccer, squash, golf, tennis and softball.

4. **Top provincial sports president:** Todd Innes, soccer.

5. **Top sports volunteer:** Bill Barron, softball.

TAKE 5: TOM HICKEY'S TOP FIVE MISCONCEPTIONS ABOUT NEWFOUNDLAND AND LABRADOR

Tom Hickey is a career politician. First elected to the House of Assembly in 1966, he held several cabinet positions until his retirement in 1986. Hickey worked in the private sector, oil industry and real estate. In 2004, he founded and was elected the president of the Newfoundland and Labrador First Party.

1. **There is a high percentage of Canadians who perceive us as the poorest province in Canada**. They don't appear to realize how rich we are in resources — both renewable and non-renewable. Those resources have been raped for the benefit of the federal government and other provinces.

2. **The majority of Canadians are ignorant of the fact that we contribute more to the Canadian economy than any other province on a per capita basis**. Research has proven this fact.

3. **Canadians generally have no perception of the significance and importance of this province to the rest of the country.** The geographic location in itself completed the coastline from sea to sea; from a defence point of view, we were necessary. Our unique culture and natural resources have made a further contribution.

4. **We are considered by too many of the national media as welfare bums who just don't want to work 12 months of the year**. Example: Margaret Wente, the *Globe and Mail* columnist who made reference to Carbonear, a place she had not even visited.

5. **We are considered by many Canadians as being backward or just plain stupid — reference typical Newfie jokes**. Most Canadians have never made an effort to get to know our people or the province.

TAKE 5: KENDRA'S LODER'S TOP FIVE WAYS TO BEAT FOG FRIZZ

Kendra Loder is an award-winning hairstylist with the Head Room in St. John's.

1. **Invest in a good ceramic flat iron**.

2. **Use an anti-humidity product**. There are many sprays that help to keep your style and block the frizz out, also shine oils can tame down frizz.

3. **Use a professional moisture shampoo and treatment** (towel dry hair, and leave on for 5-10 minutes). A lot of drugstore shampoos have the wrong Ph for your hair, which can frizz your hair before you even go outside.

4. **Wash your hair every second day instead of everyday**. This will leave behind more of your natural oils and will leave your hair more tamed.

5. **Make good colour decisions**; Make gradual changes instead of instant ones. You will be just as blond in two visits as you will in one. And if all else fails pack up and move to central Newfoundland where the salt water is far away.

TAKE 5: DALE JARVIS'S TOP FIVE SPOOKIEST PLACES IN NEWFOUNDLAND AND LABRADOR

Dale Gilbert Jarvis has been telling stories in public since 1992. One of the few professional storytellers in St. John's, the founder of the St. John's Storytelling Festival has performed at events at home and away. Dale is also the founder of the St. John's Haunted Hike (named "event of the year" by the City of St. John's). He writes a biweekly column about the paranormal for *The Telegram*; his latest book is *The Golden Leg and Other Ghostly Campfire Tales*.

1. **Victoria Street, St. John's:** Though it's one of the shorter streets in downtown St. John's (a mere three blocks), Victoria Street has more than its fair share of ghosts. One resident tells of an elderly woman who appears on the landing of his stairs. Other houses are haunted by mysterious orbs, ghostly knockings, and phantoms who open doors and run up stairways. Perhaps the eeriest haunting is a screaming spectre who appears in a bedroom — being dragged by her hair by a second ghost.

2. **Piper's Hole, Swift Current:** A ghostly piper has been playing his mournful instrument for centuries in Swift Current — his appearance has given this location its name. According to some, the phantom was an 18th-century French piper. In this version of the legend, the French and English clashed in battle at nearby Garden Cove, and the spirit of the slain Frenchman has been playing in the river valley ever since.

3. **Mockbeggar, Bonavista:** This area is the setting for a number of strange phenomena, several of which involve the Bradley House. One woman who lived in the house would hear phantom visitors walking, talking, singing, and partying at night. The area's mysteries also include a puzzling macabre discovery. In the 1920s, the influential union organizer William Coaker directed a canal to be dug near Bradley House — and the work exposed a number of coffins. Two decades later, when a bridge was being built over the same canal, more coffins were unearthed. No explanation has been found, and the graves are believed to predate the earliest cemetery in Bonavista (1725).

4. **Isle of Demons, Quirpon Island:** Stories about the Isle of Demons say that French sailors were so afraid of its devils that they would not go ashore without a crucifix in hand. Isle of Demons is thought to be Quirpon Island, at the top of the Great Northern Peninsula. It's reputation comes from a dramatic tale of love, loss, and terror involving Marguerite de Roberval, the niece of the harsh Sieur de Roberval. On her voyage from France to the New World, Marguerite aroused her uncle's wrath by becoming romantically involved with a man on the ship. When they reached Newfoundland, the Sieur de Roberval abandoned her "alone" on an island. But Marguerite found she was not alone — imps and spirits peered out of the mist, whispered in the night, and whistled in the gales. Marguerite endured for three years before her rescue and return to France.

5. **Hampden, White Bay:** The most unusual ghost in Newfoundland is the woman in white who appears along a section of road near the site of an old camp called Faulkner's Flat. Stories of the phantom began circulating in the early 1970s, but the legend may be older. Several people have seen the figure of a woman crossing the road in the area — carrying a cast-iron Waterloo stove on her back! Locals claim a woman was struck and killed by such a stove in a car accident on that stretch of road. Others identify the apparition as old Mrs. Faulkner, after whom the Flat was named.